# THE
# ODYSSEY
## OF *Winnie*

## OUR TWO-YEAR ADVENTURE OWNING AN RV

# MICHAEL MEYER

Fulton Books
Meadville, PA

Published by Fulton Books 2022

ISBN 979-8-88505-213-9 (paperback)
ISBN 979-8-88505-214-6 (digital)

Printed in the United States of America

# INTRODUCTION

If you knew how I grew up and the judgment I rained down upon "campers" most of my life, you would find it absurd to find out that I bought an RV. Now, do not get me wrong, when I saw the RV commercial of the family at the soccer tournament having freshly baked cookies, I did feel pangs of jealousy. However, most of the time when I saw an RV in the real world, the big-ass vehicle was in my way or it had that asinine Rent Me splashed across its side. Who would want to ride across the country looking like such a jackass going forty-five miles per hour down the toll road?

In spite of all this, on December 15, 2015, we purchased a thirty-five-feet-long fifteen-year-old Winnebago Adventurer 35U for about $19,000. Soon thereafter, we started driving the beast (our kids named her Winnie). The purpose of this book is to share our adventures *as I saw them*. It is my hope that my wife and daughters never read this book. Along the way, I will share what I have learned about owning an RV (for example, I learned I am a bad driver) and planning trips so that you can laugh at my mistakes and hopefully learn from them once you buy an RV. To prove the honesty of the stories, I have included pictures of our adventures.

This book will document the twenty-five-month odyssey of our RV ownership: from the genesis of the idea of getting an RV to its final sale to someone else. I will walk through all the decisions, many just plain stupid, I made along the way. Aside from opportunities to laugh at my misfortunes, these stories are designed to provide helpful hints about many things I learned. The heroes of this odyssey are Winnie and my wife, Teresa. I am probably the villain as I inflicted plenty of damage to Winnie and was kind of an a-hole to my beauti-ful, wonderful, awesome wife. Sorry about that to both of you. I am so lucky that Winnie was incredibly resilient, and Teresa has a very good sense of humor.

# THAT GUY—I WILL NEVER CAMP

I grew up in Potomac in the Maryland suburbs of Washington, DC. Over time, the rich people of Potomac decided that those of us that did not have as much money should really say we live in Rockville, Maryland. Whatever. My parents bought their house in 1965 for $28,500. It looked like all the other houses in the neighborhood, split-level generic 1960s house.

My dad worked for the government, and my mom raised the kids. When I was in grade school, my mom went to work, getting off work in time to be late picking me up from school each day. As a family, we took one vacation each year. My earliest memories were going to Ocean City, Maryland, and staying at a crappy hotel. Later, we went west to Deep Creek Lake, Maryland, for two weeks, renting a house on the lake. We would rent a boat on the lake each year. My dad trashed the boat rudder one year and had to have it replaced. More than anything, I remember how much my older sisters hated going to Deep Creek Lake.

Around 1978 (when I would have been in sixth grade), my grandfather retired and thought it would be great to own a condo in Ocean City, Maryland, so that he could go fishing whenever he wanted. He had a couple of friends in the area who owned boats, and he thought, maybe, he might get a boat as well. Except, my grandmother hated fishing and Ocean City, Maryland, and boats. So in hopes that he might get a chance to use the condo occasionally, my grandfather gave the condo to my dad and mom. From that year forward, every summer vacation was in Ocean City, Maryland.

1

The condo was a small two-bedroom apartment in a complex that consisted of twelve similarly sized apartments. The walls of each apartment as well as the floors and ceilings were made of the cheapest, thinnest materials that allowed us all to experience every step taken by the jackholes who lived above us and every conversation of those below. The condo had a unique ocean smell that might be described as *eau de seawater*. A small wooden balcony off the living room over-looked an access canal to the bay on the west side of Ocean City.

Each vacation went about the same. My brother and I would wake up early, eat something, and then head to the beach around 9:00 AM. It was about a mile walk to the beach, with one major road to cross. Once at the beach, I would toggle between body surfing and staring at girls, all the while nurturing my impending skin can-cer. Eventually, I started using some sort of sunscreen, but I think it had an SPF of 1 and had the consistency of cooking oil. I think it made me burn faster. Usually around 11:00 AM, my parents would venture over to the beach, hauling all their beach necessities: chairs, umbrella, cooler, inflatable rafts, etc. In spite of my dad's portly fea-tures, he would still enjoy the ocean, floating on the raft just outside of the breaking waves. I have to hand it to that guy…big belly, hairy back, and no shirt while at the beach. I think now he would be sued for causing emotional damage, back then nobody cared. Lunch con-sisted of sand-covered sandwiches. Of course, they were not made that way, but once you take the sandwich with a hand covered in sand, it might as well have been made of sand.

Around 3:00 PM, we would head home with all our gear. I remember one day we were waiting to cross Route 50 (the one major road) and my dad had the beach umbrella over his shoulder. He turned to talk to Mom and whacked some lady across the side of her head with the umbrella. She went down and was a bit groggy. These days, Dad would be in prison for such an offense, but back then, the lady got back up and went on her way. Once home, Mom and Dad would get to drinking. They liked having a daiquiri, piña colada, or gin and tonic. They would make us a daiquiri sans alcohol. Then Mom would get out the cheese and crackers, possibly some shrimp or crab claws, and we would just chill.

Later in the evening, after dinner, my brother and I would go down to the end of the boardwalk, which was about thirty blocks away, about two and a half miles. We would ride the bus down to the end of the boardwalk, then walk home since the busses were too crowded on the way home. There were plenty of arcade games to play. They also had rides, but we could not afford to ride on them. Only the rich kids and the teenagers could have that kind of fun. Besides the arcades, I remember standing by a dunk tank with a guy dressed as a clown, insulting anyone who tried to throw a baseball at the target. Sometimes he would get the thrower so mad there would be threats and balls thrown at the cage, but mostly I laughed at the insults because they were funny and because they were not hurled at me.

Some days, we would help with the yard work around the condo with Dad. We would trim these horrid pricker bushes or mow the grass. Everyone at the condo was too cheap to pay for someone to do this, so the upkeep was left to the residents who generally did not give a crap and refused to use up their vacation doing yard work. Dad always paid us for our time, which provided a source of funds to blow at the arcades.

Until I went to college, I thought everyone's summer vacations were like mine—always at the ocean (I had long since put the dark years of Deep Creek Lake behind me), somewhere on the East Coast. When I went to college in the Midwest, I realized not everyone went to the ocean. In fact, many folks would go to one of the many lakes that speckle the Midwest. I could not fathom how awful those experiences must have been. I remember hearing my roommate telling me about their family vacation house on the coast of Lake Huron. I actually visited the house once but was not told that they did not have hot water or air-conditioning until I arrived. Any bathing had to take place with a bar of soap in Lake Huron. My snooty Potomac, Maryland, sensibilities did not appreciate this form of camping. To add insult to injury, the shoreline of Lake Huron had rocks instead of sand. Thus, to get out to wash, my sensitive feet had trouble negotiating the shoreline, both on the way in and out. No doubt, I am a colossal pussy.

My wife's family, on the other hand, seemed to have lots of adventures camping. Get this…they would sleep in a tent. What the hell? In fact, my wife and her whole family love to tell stories of when they drove across the country in a station wagon. Starting in Atlanta, Georgia, they drove across the country all the way to California and back, pitching a tent and sleeping outside every night. No air-conditioning. No amenities. No thanks. Even after my wife graduated from college, she would go camping and sleep in tents outside. As a family, we once tried to sleep outside in our side yard. Our daughters were little (Addison and Lily were six, and Kelsey was four). At some point, one of the twins wanted to go inside (because nature was too loud), and I jumped at the opportunity to get the hell out of the tent and sleep in my bed, with the comfort of air-conditioning to nourish a joyful happy night of restful sleep. My wife and one of my daughters lasted the night and woke tired and haggard.

Ironically, my favorite TV shows involve people trying to survive in the wilderness or people trying to dig for gold. I have to be honest, if I were ever in a survival situation, I am confident I would die an early death. On one episode of *Alone*, some dude bailed in the first couple of hours. That would be me. I am in awe of those with real survival skills, though it seems, they would rarely come in handy given my chosen profession—teaching accounting. One of my daughters mentioned a few days ago that the opposite of magic is accounting. Great to be the butt of an eleven-year-old's joke. I just do not understand why someone would venture out into the wilderness, knowing that they are going to have to live on beetles and their own pee.

# EVOLUTION

I did not wake up one day and think, *I need an RV*. My thinking evolved, spurred on mostly by an uninformed analysis of the costs and benefits of owning an RV. It all started with Addison being semi-obsessed with dinosaurs. When I was a kid, there were five kinds of dinosaurs: T. rex, stegosaurus, triceratops, brontosaurus, and pterodactyl. As I grew older, I learned of one additional dinosaur (velociraptor) because of *Jurassic Park* and because of the Toronto NBA franchise. I thought that was a pretty thorough understanding of the dinosaur world until my daughter started doing research into dinosaurs. She would sit in her room and read the *Dinosaur Encyclopedia* for hours. I started having heated exchanges when she would mention a dinosaur name, and I would say "does not exist, never did" because it made no sense that in a relatively short period of time, there would suddenly be hundreds of different dinosaurs. To make matters worse, some dino-jackholes decided that brontosauruses never existed and pterodactyls must be called pterosaurs and were not dinosaurs but reptiles.

So my wife, Teresa, and I started talking about whether there might be some opportunity to dig for dinosaur fossils so as to help foster Addison's interest. In hindsight, it kind of seems stupid to burn so many calories on the interests of a seven-year-old. We discovered that the Children's Museum in Indianapolis has a program where families go out with paleontologists and dig for fossils (google "Wyoming Dinosaur Adventure"). Except, you do not get to keep the fossils. Families are free labor and then sent on their way. And there is no guarantee that you actually find any fossils. That seemed

5

like a sucker arrangement. Thanks to a bit of Internet searching, I was able to find a site in southwestern Wyoming where you dig for and get to keep almost all the fossils you can find.

At this point, I really have no idea what happened. How did a casual conversation about what we might want to do someday change, or shall we say evolve, into a much bigger deal? I say I have no idea what happened, but I know exactly what happened. My beautiful, wonderful, awesome wife looked at a map and saw a whole bunch of other stuff we could see if we traveled to Wyoming. Or perhaps she had been planning for years how to go on a trip like this and sprang into action like a ninja-Jedi-master confronted by some hairy dullard. We could see the Badlands, Mount Rushmore, Devils Tower, Yellowstone, and Grand Teton on our way to hunt for fossils. My initial response when someone presents me with such a change in plans (especially when they are so different from my own) is to dismiss the idea as really stupid and impossible. I mean, come on. We struggle going to visit my parents on a ten-hour trip in our minivan. How is a much longer trip going to go? Oh, wait, I know how it is going to go. Really, really, really, really, F——cking badly.

Teresa was not surprised by my reaction. She knew I was going to be against anything new. So she sowed the seeds and walked away…letting the seeds germinate. In the meantime, my head was exploding. I did not want to let her down, but I did not want to do this. It was not in my plan. But Teresa said nothing; she just let it go. Pretty sure I got played.

Eventually, my "not gonna do it" transformed to "how we gonna do it." Step 1, we simply could not take our minivan. I think Teresa may have whispered "RV" in my ear while I slept, but one day, it dawned on me that the only way we could do this was if we rented an RV for the trip. Maybe it could be fun, as long as we had air-conditioning. I am not sleeping outside or anywhere without air-conditioning. So again, with the help of the Internet, there are ways to figure out how much it costs to rent an RV. It seemed like there were two options: rent a crappy RV for a lot of money or rent a nice RV for even more money. Of course, the devil was in the details, and all of the details seemed to add up to even more money. It seemed like there were three big rental charges: charges per day, plus a charge per mile, and a charge to use the generator. Doing a little bit of math, it seemed like this trip was going to cost more than $3,500 without considering the cost of gas or anything else.

Then I thought, *What if I were to buy a "beater" RV? We could use it and then sell it. If I lost less than $3,500 on the transaction, then I would come out on top.*

At first, I kept the beater concept to myself as I had no idea how to broach the subject with Teresa. For all I knew, she may have forgotten about going on this trip. But I became obsessed with finding that perfect "beater"—working, cheap, and not likely to decrease much more in value.

As a sidenote, in our family, we have separate functions. As an accountant, I am the CFO (chief financial officer) while Teresa is the CEO (chief executive officer). So, in the end, she makes the big decisions. These titles became necessary as a consequence of our first important decision as a married couple.

FLASHBACK: Before we got married, Teresa lived in Atlanta, and I lived in New Orleans. Because of my job, Teresa agreed to come live in New Orleans after we got married. A few months before the wedding, she came over to New Orleans, and we went looking for a house. I had suggested that we live in Slidell, a northeastern suburb of New Orleans as it seemed nicer than the homes we could afford closer to the city. I already owned a house in Metairie, but it had a very small backyard. The yard was important because my wife came with two large redbone coonhounds.

After an exhaustive search of homes, at one point, my wife asked, "So why do you want to live in Slidell?"

The home we had just viewed was a great party house. It had a pool with a large backyard and a large hot tub in the garage, though we kind of had a feeling they filmed porn in the house. We finally found a neighborhood we liked (my wife liked) but did not find a house we liked that we could afford. So I would check the Internet and drive around the neighborhood on occasion before we got married to see if any new homes came on the market. Finally, a home came on the market that seemed ideal. By *ideal*, I mean it had a large backyard. So I took a tour, took pictures, and asked for her input. She thought it was fine if I thought we should buy it. As time was an issue because of multiple offers, I decided, without her seeing the house, to buy it.

Right after our honeymoon, we went back to Atlanta to pack up her stuff in a U-Haul and drove as a married couple to our new home.

As we turned into the driveway, my wife's first comment was, "So…the driveway is not paved…"

This was just the beginning of the bad.

Next, we walked into the home, and my wife said, "They were smokers!"

Because my wife has asthma, this lingering cigarette smell was causing her to have trouble breathing. F——CK!

It seemed like a bad timing, but I noted, "Have you seen the backyard?"

We ended up taking every wooden object out of the house and sealing it with Kilz. We did the same with all of the wooden cabinets in the kitchen. We replaced all of the baseboard molding and changed out the carpet that was not already new. We painted every wall as well. I will ignore the fact that the city refused to turn on our electricity because they said we needed a new septic system, though my dumb-f——ck asswipe home inspector said that we were hooked up to city sewage. And it was August. We lived at my old house in Metairie until we could get the electricity turned on and the stink out.

I fully admit my mistake was buying a house that my wife had not inspected and approved. You should never buy a house because of the backyard. I see douchebags make this mistake on HGTV all the time. Because of this mistake, we decided that all major decisions should be approved by my wife. I can determine if we can afford it, but in the end, my decision-making often is not the best. This reminds me of another bad decision I made before we were married. After I moved to Metairie, I realized I needed an SUV that was higher off the ground. I was on my way to work one day, and for no particular reason, a rainstorm sat over New Orleans, dumping about six inches of water in an hour. Some streets were flooded, including the parking lot at the University of New Orleans where I worked. The roads leading onto the campus had more than six inches of rainwater flowing over them. At that point, I realized my Mazda generic four-door piece of shit was probably going to stall out, and I needed something with bigger tires. I liked the look and feel of the Nissan Xterra, so I decided to buy one. At the dealer, I drew a line in the sand on what I was going to pay. I refused to pay an additional $1,500 for the electric package. When I told my soon-to-be wife of my purchase, she could not stop laughing.

"You mean you have to crank down the windows? I did not even know they made those kinds of cars anymore."

For an additional $25 dollars a month, I could have had electric everything. Instead, I had electric nothing. I showed them.

My future wife remarked, "You make bad decisions."

In hindsight, she should have known I was going to screw up the house buying decision given my Xterra negotiation. So, yeah, my wife makes the major decisions.

I started my search for the perfect combination of inexpensive and nice used RV on Craigslist. I would spend hours looking for RVs for sale near Northern Indiana. Having exhausted the possibilities here, I expanded the search area to Chicago, Detroit, Indianapolis, Columbus, etc. Of course, I still had not broached the subject with my wife about buying an RV, but I continued searching before bed almost every night. At some point, I stumbled upon a different website, RVTrader.com. This website had better offerings as many of the RVs were being sold by dealers and not individuals. However, with *nicer* came a bigger price tag. And, at the time, I had kept my budget to below $10,000.

I finally grew a pair and mentioned the financial benefits of buying an RV versus renting to the CEO. Much to my surprise, Teresa agreed that this would be a reasonable financial decision. However, my use of the word *beater* seemed to be a sticking point.

Her response to the use of the term *beater* was, "I am not going in a *beater*."

She went on to describe her requirements on a potential RV. None of those things she described could possibly be included in a "beater." I think in her mind she was thinking about an RV that a friend drove to our house two years in a row for the first Notre Dame football game of the season. It was large. It had slide-outs (the living room and bedroom expanded out when parked), a large kitchen, nice bathroom, etc. Needless to say, there were no RVs for sale in my price range that had the amenities that she required…the budget had to increase. It turns out you can spend a shit load of money on an RV if you wish.

One of my friends at work was discussing that he golfed with someone who was very much into the RV lifestyle. Given my complete lack of knowledge, I asked for his name and emailed him asking for advice. He recommended that my wife and I stop by his tailgater before a football game to get a tour of their RV, and he would be happy to provide any assistance he could give. One thing my wife and I realized when we moved to northern Indiana, Midwest people are really, really nice. Some days, I am afraid that I might get kicked out if my former east coast douchebag qualities start seeping through. We met Bill and his wife, Michelle, at their tailgater. They provided lots of sound advice, and I will share it below:

1. You want an RV with levelers. They keep the RV steady and level when parked. And not all RV parks are level, so levelers assure that you do not have to sleep at an angle.
2. You want an oven. Some RVs do not have an oven, just a cooktop and a convection microwave. The oven is key for those cookies and for cooking in general.
3. You want slide-outs to make it more livable while parked. It really adds space.
4. No shitting in the RV. Better to pull over and shit at a rest stop than deal with floating dookies that can splash about and cause a major stink.

5.  Before buying a used RV, make sure the outside skin is not peeling off (delaminating). Look for sides bubbling out. It can be a sign of structural problems with the RV that may be unrepairable.
6.  Check tires and awnings. This can be a significant cost to replace. New is better than old.
7.  Make sure the generator oil filter is readily accessible. Smaller generators can be hard to maintain.
8.  If there is a rooftop air conditioner, look for signs of water leaking.

# MAKING THE PURCHASE

**A**rmed with this advice, I resumed my search for used RVs on the RVTrader website. I set my top budget at $20,000. I was able to narrow my search to three RVs: One was at a dealership outside of Detroit, one was at a dealership in Columbus, Ohio, and one was at a dealership south of Toledo, Ohio. No offense to anyone in the sales industry, but I have lots of baggage when it comes to dealing with salespeople. Maybe it was my first car buying experience where, in hindsight, I believe I was cornholed. I carry a big grudge against salespeople. Given their incentive system, they are concerned about their commission, not me. So the less interaction I have to have with a salesperson, the better off I will be. Rather than making phone calls, which I hate to do, I emailed each of the three dealerships in the order of the RVs I was interested in.

The first contact was to the dealership in Columbus, Ohio. They had a 2000 Winnebago Adventurer 35U. This model had two slide-outs, levelers, an oven, and a big enough generator and slept six. There appeared to be some damage to the passenger seat, but otherwise, it seemed in okay shape. The selling price was what put his baby on top of my list—listed for sale at just under $16,000. I thought that there was little room for it to fall in value, thus little chance I was going to lose much on the deal. Alas, they never responded to my email. Seriously, what the hell? Nice effort. Moving on.

After a week of waiting for a response from the dumbass Columbus RV dealership, I sent an email to the second dealership outside of Detroit. I forget what brand the RV was, but it had one feature the Winnebago did not: a washer/dryer. That seemed like a

12

nice option. This RV was smaller but seemed nicer—and was more expensive. They were asking around $20,000. My email informed them that I lived four hours away from them and did not want to travel to haggle. I needed to know their bottom price before I set off to look at it in person. I received a response, which I felt was a victory. However, that feeling was short-lived when I read the email, and it said they wanted me to call their salesperson. Is it too damn hard for you, who want my cash in exchange for an RV you want to sell, to just email me the information I asked for—or at least have the salesperson contact me in person? Eat shit. Moving on.

With great trepidation, I contacted the third RV dealer outside of Toledo, Ohio. They also had a 2000 Winnebago Adventurer 35U. There appeared to be some damage to the floor near the dining table but no other apparent damage. They were asking $19,900. I sent a similar email asking for the best price because it was three hours to drive. I received a response back within an hour. They knocked $1,000 off the price. I told him that we would come over to look at the coach that next weekend. Here is a free lesson to budding sales-people: If you want the sale, actually contact the customer. You are welcome.

I had already contacted our credit union to have a preapproved loan for no more than $20,000. Trying to find loans for less expensive RVs proved to be more of a calorie burn than I had hoped it would be. We have been able to refinance our house (to get lower rates) multiple times almost entirely online. Somehow, a smaller loan was a bridge too far for some financial institutions. I realize that values of RVs drop, but surely someone should be able to come up with a simpler process. Many banks will not finance RVs, and most of the online services want you to buy a $100,000-plus RV in order for them to deem it worth their time. To dissuade you from using their service, they offer ridiculous rates. While I was not super pleased with the 6.5-percent rate my credit union offered, it was the lowest rate I could find for the value of RV I wanted to purchase. But my plan was to only own the thing for a few months, so it was not going to be a huge burden. Here comes the accountant...note that the interest on RVs we were looking at qualified to be deductible for tax purposes. There are requirements on what amenities the RV must have to qualify, so consult your tax professional. Or use Google. Basically, if it has a kitchen, bathroom, and bedroom, it is considered a home. You are welcome.

Early the next Saturday, the family jumped into our minivan and headed to middle of nowhere, Ohio, to look at the RV. I am unsure what anyone else in the car was thinking, but I was hoping this was going to end with us owning an RV. With financing secured and what seemed like the family CEO on board, we just had to make sure there were no significant problems with the coach. When we got to the dealership, my anus was puckered. As mentioned earlier, I have a genuine dislike for salespeople.

FLASHBACK: It all dates back to my experience buying a Ford Mustang just after I graduated from college. I found the car I liked, and I realized the sales douchebags knew I wanted the car and were playing every game possible with me. All I needed to do was walk away and go to a different dealership, and all would have been fine. I wanted the Ford Mustang convertible with the 5.0-liter engine. Douchebag dealership had a beautiful black one with a white convertible roof. After test-driving the car (it had a manual transmission which made it so much more fun to drive), I knew I needed this car. But I was not in a position at that point to make the purchase. In spite of this, I felt like I was trapped in the dealership for hours. I harbor so much anger over spending that time trapped in that dealership. I forget the name of the dealership, but it was next to Montgomery Mall in Bethesda, Maryland. If any of the sales staff are reading this book, allow me to say, EAT SHIT!

Anyway, because of this scarring over my first car purchase, I dread going into any environment where salespeople are getting paid a commission. However, to my complete surprise, all of the people at this RV dealership could not have been less hands-on. They told us to look in all the RVs on the lot. They had moved the one we were interested in buying up front but had unlocked all the RVs on the lot and allowed us to walk through them all. My daughters especially liked going in the new ones and guessing how much they would cost.

All of them were over $70,000, with a few over $100,000. After touring all of the RVs, the one we were there to see seemed rather modest and small. We then asked for a test-drive. The salesperson assumed that I had some experience driving large vehicles. Nope.

SALESPERSON: Does your family like to camp?
ME: No.
SALESPERSON: Have you owned a travel trailer or fifth wheel?
ME: Nope.
SALESPERSON: So…have you driven any RV before? Rented a Class C?
ME: Nope.
SALESPERSON: You know, most people work their way up to a Class A coach.
ME: Not us.
SALESPERSON: Have you ever driven any large vehicle?
ME: I have driven a moving van.
SALESPERSON: Silence…

As perplexed as the salesperson was of my experience, I think he was most baffled by my insistence that I did not camp. As I have stated before, I am not someone who camps, ever, anywhere, for any reason.

Before the test-drive started, I asked if the salesperson could drive for a little while so I could watch him and pick up any pointers as we cruised down the road. And that was what we did. Upon pulling out of the parking lot, we discovered that the flat-screen TV perched between the driver and passenger was not bolted down. The first bump out of the parking lot caused the TV to flop down and nearly smash the face of the salesperson. I kind of caught it and was able to hold it until we could pull over, get its cords unscrewed, and set it safely on the ground. I am so glad he was driving. With the TV secured, we went down the road a few miles, pulled into a large empty parking lot and switched drivers. I drove back to the RV dealership. My comment to my wife was that it was no more difficult to drive than a minivan[1]. This is the type of statement that will, in time, come back to bite me. Believe it or not, my wife has an amazing memory for such statements. After the test-drive, we decided we needed to have a family meeting. I asked for a poll of who wanted to purchase the RV. Unanimous. I tried to dive a little deeper, letting everyone know that we would be living in the RV. One daughter thought that we would be driving this between hotels. Once it was clarified that there would be no hotel, a second vote was taken, with a more tepid unanimous vote. So I went into the dealership, paid a deposit, signed some paperwork, and *boom*. We owned an RV.

The dealership was great. They wanted to make sure all systems were in working order. It was apparent that a new set of tires was needed, so we went ahead and purchased a new set of six tires for what seemed like a really reasonable price. The dealer agreed to replace all of the awnings as well (they were in a terrible state). A couple of weeks later, we went to pick up the coach. The dealer wanted the entire family there as we were going to get a lesson on how everything worked. Their idea was that one person will forget most things. However, with five sets of ears, maybe everyone will remember something. We had a one-and-half-hour lesson on how the plumbing system, electrical systems, entertainment systems, propane gas systems, kitchen systems, bathroom systems, awnings systems, etc. worked. Matt, the RV guru who showed us all the stuff also, was willing to be on call in case we needed him…which we did. With the lesson complete, paperwork signed, check exchanged, keys handed over, and temporary license plate attached, it was ours. My thought was simple: *What the hell have I gotten myself into?*

On the way out of town, we stopped at a Bob Evans Restaurant which allowed me to focus on the task at hand: get this damn thing home without breaking it or getting into an accident. One of the minor details I had not considered was the passenger-side side window was a bit fogged. I noticed the window during the test-drive, but I assumed that it was caused by warm people in a cold RV. Apparently I was wrong. It was caused by a fifteen-year-old double-pane window

---

[1]    Ironically, we own a Honda Odyssey.

with a bad seal. Of course, looking out the side window is critical to see the side mirror which is critical to making sure you have enough room to slide over when passing a car or truck. I also never noticed how narrow the toll booths were on the Ohio and Indiana toll roads. I learned that I really needed to get the E-ZPass attached to the windshield. I had to have my daughter crawl up onto the dashboard and hold the E-ZPass up high as we passed through the toll booths. So glad the wife did not see that. I also learned rather quickly that this RV was a giant rectangle on wheels that caught the wind like a giant sail. Since there are no hills or trees to stop the wind anywhere in Western Ohio or Northern Indiana, lane management on the toll road was a challenge. It really was nothing like driving a minivan, but I did not want to let my wife know. She was miles ahead driving the minivan home. Not to worry, my daughters would tell her everything that I did, especially the stuff that might fall under the category of "bad" parenting.

# GOTTA HAVE A NAME

The beauty of having three daughters is that they like to name stuff. They must have had over seventy stuffed animals, and each had its own name. This leads to fun games like "where is Dolphy?" Who is Dolphy? A crappy, barely stuffed dolphin that we "won" at a cannot-lose carny game at the boardwalk in Ocean City, Maryland (that cost me $5). Apparently, it was more important than the six or seven other stuffed dolphins we had.

In any event, once we purchased the RV, the girls decided the RV needed a name. My memory suggests that my wife may have been the catalyst to the naming process. After some deliberation, the family agreed to henceforth call the RV Winnie. And so I will do in kind.

# OBJECTS APPEAR SMALLER THAN THEY ACTUALLY ARE

Aside from the pangs of fear getting through the toll booths, driving Winnie was exhilarating. But it still seemed like there should be some driving pointers given before they hand over the keys. I mean, they just shook my hand, thanked me for the business, and sent me on my way. Maybe if you are going to give an hour-and-a-half tutorial on flushing the toilet and putting down the awning, you might cut out a little time to explain that driving an RV is NOT like driving a minivan. My test-drive consisted of me driving straight down a road about three miles. Maybe a little discussion that if you turn sharply, the back of the RV is going to swing out and potentially take out a gas pump or your neighbor. Or perhaps a little discussion about how tall the RV is so that you can confidently go under an overpass without puckering. I promise, later in the book, I will share details of what I learned about driving the RV so that you can avoid some of my very expensive mistakes.

Eventually, I got Winnie home. Both my wife and I were quite surprised to find that Winnie took up our entire driveway. It seemed so small relative to the other RVs on the lot I never considered that it was still a big-ass RV. I needed to get Winnie as far over to the side of our driveway as possible so that we might be able to get our cars out of our garage. In between our driveway and our neighbor's driveway, there were these old (quite ugly) pine trees. In attempting to move as far over in the driveway as I could, I ended up raking the RV against a bunch of branches. As I inched forward, I could hear this screeching noise as the branches brushing against and eventually leaving nice scratches on Winnie's side. Because of this, I decided to trim back all the branches off Winnie to protect the big girl from future damage. This was the first of many mistakes and miscalculations I made. Rather than trimming the branches back to the tree trunk, I just cut off enough so they were not touching Winne. There she sat until I could find a more permanent place to park her. Our homeowners association did not allow RVs to be parked in driveways, so I needed to act fast.

*Figure 1. Winnie takes up our entire driveway. This was taken just as we arrived from purchasing Winnie.*

Northern Indiana is the home of the RV Hall of Fame and home to a number of large RV manufacturers. So I thought there would be hundreds of places I could park Winnie. Close to where we lived, there were a few places, but many of them seemed a bit dodgy. For example, there was a farmer who would let people park their RVs and boats in one of his fields. Seemed like a perfect place to allow mice or vagrants to move into Winnie, and I did not want either of those things to happen. On the other end of the spectrum, there was a converted sporting goods store that was an indoor RV storage lot. However, I really wanted to be able to access Winnie whenever I wanted, and this was not possible here. Plus they did not have any spaces available. And had they had any, those spaces were expensive. I eventually found a paved, fenced in-lot that I would have 24-7 access to Winnie that was about fourteen miles from our house. The space was not covered, but it seemed safe. The cost of $60 per month seemed reasonable.

Having secured a spot for Winnie, I went to move her over to her new home. I jumped behind the wheel. The girls wanted to ride in Winnie too. We were all kind of excited. Then I put Winnie in reverse. Not having trimmed the branches back enough, as I backed up, one of the branches got lodged in the side-view mirror and snapped off part of the plastic surrounding the side-view mirror. If you are keeping score, in my driveway, I was able to scratch Winnie's side panel and break the casing surrounding the side-view mirror (on the driver's side). The best thing about my family was how funny they found these mistakes.

Once I got Winnie to her new home (SafeLock Storage, Elkhart, Indiana), I started thinking about all of the snow we get in Northern Indiana in the winter. We are near enough to Lake Michigan that we average about seventy inches of snow a year, much of which is lake effect snow. I did not know if there was a leak in the roof, and if snow was going to pile up on its roof, damage would occur before I would know about it. I decided I needed to get a cover for Winnie. And, yes, they have giant covers for RVs, and I bought mine off the Internet after a bit of googling. It is one thing to get a cover for an RV, and it is another thing, as I soon found out, to put said cover on an RV. The weekend after the cover arrived, my wife and I set off to put this waterproof blanket on our Winnie. Having read the directions and unpacked the cover, my wife had compassion on my befuddled face and provided some guidance on how she thought it should go. She has an engineering degree and is generally much better at this sort of puzzle. Eventually, our plan was for me to drape the end of the cover over my shoulders, climb to the roof of the RV, and slip the cover over Winnie. For the most part, she was right, except that I had not considered the fact that there was a radio antenna sticking up from the roof. Once we figured that out, all seemed fine. All I needed to do was walk to the back of Winnie and climb down the ladder. I did not take into consideration that there were all sorts of things on Winnie's roof. For example, there was a satellite dish, a solar panel, several hatches that allow for venting, and a domed translucent plastic ceiling for the bathroom. Though I thought I was being careful, I stepped on the domed translucent ceiling for the bathroom, making a distinct sound of cracking plastic. F——ck. I do not think I told my wife I did that. We just tied the cover down and left.

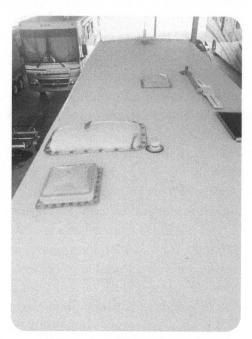

*Figure 2. Picture of Winnie's roof. Note the crack on the white domed cover that was repaired with a little silicone caulk. The fact was that the domed cover already had two cracks, and me stepping on it simply broke the seal of a previous repair. I did not make a new crack.*

# HELPFUL HINT: TURNING AN RV

I put this helpful hint first because this is the one piece of knowledge I wish I had. In fact, I am a bit perplexed that the RV salesperson and/or Matt (the RV guru) did not let me in on this little secret. Watch how you turn. Depending on the size of the RV, the back wheels can either follow the front wheels or they can act as a fulcrum which causes the back of the RV to swing out wide. If your goal is to destroy all things in your wake, feel free to turn sharply. If, however, you want to keep from paying for significant repairs, always be aware of where the back end of your RV is going.

The tail end of Winnie extends about twelve and a half feet beyond the back tires. That means anything in a twelve-and-a-half-foot radius of my back tires is in the death zone if I were to make a tight turn. I cannot tell you how many gas pumps I almost slammed because I did not know this simple driving tip as I pulled away from the pumps.

As an exercise, take a pen or pencil and set it on a table. Place your finger about one-third down the pencil. Rotate the pencil around your finger, pushing from the longer side. Look how the back part of the pencil rotates out as the pencil rotates. That is the back of your RV, hitting stuff.

If you have a new RV, go to an open parking lot. Have your significant other stand next to the RV, near the back. Crank on the steering wheel, turning away from your significant other. Watch how the back of the RV hits your significant other if they do not get out of the way. Then, have your significant other sit next to you every time you turn the wheel while driving, and I am confident they will remind you that you almost ran them over. It might just be better than an alarm.

Note that not all RVs will have this problem. The placement of the rear tires is about weight distribution. In our RV, the engine was up front, so the rear tires were placed to balance the rest of the RV. For RVs with a rear engine (known as pushers), the placement of the rear tires is under the engine, so this is a nonissue.

# LET'S TAKE WINNIE

Our normal Christmas trip takes us to visit my parents who live in the Maryland suburbs of Washington, DC, specifically Potomac, Maryland (my childhood home). Because we had just purchased Winnie, we thought it would be fun to take her rather than the minivan. There was a whole array of things that probably needed to be done to prepare for this trip, but we were just using it as a vehicle to drive. So why pretend like we were going to camp. I think the only thing I did to prepare Winnie was put some water in the holding tank and put some toilet treatment liquid in the toilet. The rule was no shitting in Winnie. I had no idea how to operate anything in Winnie, but I did flip through the 126 page operating manual thinking, *Man, there is a lot of stuff to know.*

Arming ourselves with blankets and pillows, we loaded into Winnie in the early morning of December 27. About thirty seconds after pulling onto the Indiana Toll Road, the coffeepot shook loose and smashed into a billion little shards of glass on the floor. I just kept driving, leaving my wife to clean up the mess. No big deal. Neither of us drink coffee.

The normal ten-hour drive took twelve, but otherwise, it was fine. I did not need to make many turns and had not destroyed any gas pumps as we refilled Winnie at a rest stop in Pennsylvania (straight in, straight out). A day after arriving at my parents' house, we got a call from our dog sitter saying that the power was off, and she was leaving. Shit. So we had to cut our trip short to get back to our dogs.

We left early the next morning. While we were frustrated by the dog-sitting situation that cut our visit to Grandma and Grandpa's house short, Winnie seemed to be doing just fine. Driving her was a piece of cake, though she did struggle a bit going over the mountains, and it was a bit scary when going through road construction zones. Having been through about a dozen toll booths by now, my level of concern going through them had diminished as I would just use the wider booths designed for the trucks. Upon leaving the Pennsylvania Turnpike and entering the Ohio Turnpike, I thought nothing of going through the toll booth. Until I heard a crash. Turning to my right, the right side mirror had nearly smashed through the side window and was looking a bit sad with the mirror parts dangling by wires.

ME: What was that?
ADDISON (who was sitting in the passenger seat): Did you not see the sign?
ME: What sign?
ADDISON: The sign that said watch both mirrors.
ME: No!
ADDISON: Ha ha ha ha ha ha ha…
THE REST OF THE FAMILY: Ha ha ha ha ha ha ha…

I pulled over at the first rest stop, which was only about two miles away to survey the damage. Yep, I had broken the side mirrors. Inside the rest stop, I got a roll of duct tape. I taped the shit out of the mirrors so they stayed put for the remainder of the trip, though they were completely shattered. As I mentioned before, the side mirrors are really important to safely change lanes. There is a rear-facing camera that acts as a rearview mirror, but not having the passenger side mirror made driving sketchier than normal. Good thing I am such an excellent driver—way to go, Rainman.

*Figure 3. Back side of smashed mirror where you can see impact zone.*

*Figure 4. Front of smashed mirror with shattered glass*
*and duct tape holding lower mirror in place.*

I was able to find online a used side mirror, which I replaced myself. This was just a simple repair. A couple of screws, clip a few wires attaching the old mirror, connect wires for the new mirror and *boom*, fixed. The new mirror did not adjust electronically as it had before but no big deal. I was sure it would be fine.

# THE FIRST OFFICIAL TRIP

**A**s winter merged into spring, we decided it would be fun to try out Winnie and go on a short trip during our daughters' spring break. The plan was for me to drive the girls in Winnie and my wife to follow us in our minivan down to Indianapolis—about a three-hour trip. There was a KOA camping site where we could test our retention from Matt's (the RV guru) one-and-a-half-hour orientation.

Picking up Winnie and bringing her home went without incident. The branches had been cut away from the driveway to keep from repeating the issues I had last time I parked this monstrosity in our driveway. We spent the better part of a week getting everything ready and outfitting Winnie with plates, silverware, pots, pans, glasses, etc.

Unlike our quick trip to Maryland in December, this was going to be a real trip, and Winnie needed to be prepared. There were a few systems that needed to be primed before we could leave. Everything you need to know was in the operations manual for the RV. Read this as many times as you can. Ours was 126 pages and had pictures to show you what to look for and lots of step-by-step instructions. First, I wanted to get the refrigerator cold. We plugged Winnie via extension cord to our outside plug which allowed the electrical system to function. Next, the plumbing system needed to be flushed of the antifreeze that was in the pipes from the winterizing process, and I needed to put some toilet treatment liquid in the toilet (it helps break down the gross stuff and keeps the stink to a minimum). I purchased a lot of this along with RV-approved toilet paper from Amazon.

When the day arrived for our departure, I was excited. Down Route 31 we went from Granger, Indiana (near South Bend), first stop to be the Indianapolis KOA. It was somewhat of a windy day, but nothing this expert driver could not handle.

About forty miles south of South Bend, I got a call on my cell phone from my wife.

TERESA: Pull over.
ME: Why?
TERESA: Look in the mirrors.
ME: Oh, shit.

I heard a banging sound, looked in the side mirrors, and saw what appeared to be wings. As it turned out, not wings but a couple of the cargo doors were flapping wide open. Luckily none of our crap had dumped out along Route 31. So the first stop was actually the shoulder of Route 31 where I learned a valuable lesson. Lock the damn cargo doors. After solving that issue, we were back on the road.

As I drove, I kept wondering to myself how RV parks work. This was going to be a new experience, and I had no idea what to expect. How dodgy might it be? Will it be obvious that I have no idea what I am doing? Pulling into the RV park, there were plenty of signs that clearly told me where to go. As I parked and walked into the office, I was greeted with incredibly nice and helpful people. They were going to get in a golf cart and take me to my spot. This seemed idiotproof, which is good because all evidence to date regarding Winnie would indicate I am an idiot.

Once at our spot, I looked around, and there were only a few RVs parked. It was late March, so it seemed reasonable that not very many people would be camping. It was helpful because there were several critical tasks to perform, and I could look at the other RVs for hints: (1) plug into the electrical outlets at our parking spot, (2) hook up the water system from a spigot at our parking spot to our RV, and (3) level the RV.

There were three plug options which was confusing to me at first, but upon examining my plug and the plug options, it seemed obvious which one to use—the one that fits. Flip the switch on and *boom*—we have power to Winnie. Task number 2 was a bit more of a challenge because the waterline hose we had in Winnie was nonexistent. I did not have a waterline hose. No one told me to have one. So I walked back to the KOA office which also doubled as a snack bar, swallowed my pride, and asked them if they sold waterline hoses. Of course, they did. Back at Winnie, I screwed in the hose to Winnie, and the other end to a water spigot, opened the spigot, and *boom*, we have water pressure.

Lastly, I needed to level Winnie. I went through the steps I recalled Matt (the RV Guru) telling me (and I reviewed the operating manual several dozen times), and sure enough, the levelers dropped down. I found a bubble level in the console left by the previous owners and used it to make sure we were all level. *Boom*. I am an RV expert. Nothing could go wrong; I am the best.

Our plan was to make dinner in Winnie's kitchen. You know, if we are going to camp, let's camp. Unfortunately, the first order of business was to open a can, and we did not have a can opener. In addition, we did not have a pan big enough to cook our dinner (we were going to make tacos). So I did a little Google search and found the closest Walmart (a recurring theme in our RV adventures) and purchased a can opener; a pot; a pan; and, I think, some ice cream. After dinner, we watched a movie together on the flat-screen TV (including cooking popcorn in the microwave), then decided to shower and turn in for the night. We were going to shower in the KOA showers, and I admit, I was a bit concerned it was going to be a bit dodgy. Nope, wrong, again. The bathrooms and showers were very clean, and everyone was in a good mood and ready for sleep. We had purchased foam mattress cushions to go over all of the beds. Everything was extremely comfortable but a bit cold. The last new experience of the day was to get the furnace working, which I did. I am an RV expert. I am the best. This camping stuff is a piece of cake.

The next day, we headed off for our spring break in the minivan. Not that it is important to the RV story, but we spent one of the days in French Lick. French Lick is best known as the home of Larry Bird, famous NBA player with the Boston Celtics who went by the nickname the Hick from French Lick. Not too far from French Lick is an elephant rescue where we got to get up close and personal with some African elephants (Wilstem Wildlife Park). My wife and I got to wash an elephant, and my daughters got to give an elephant a pedicure. We also went to a water park in French Lick and the Children's Museum in Indianapolis. All in all, a very successful spring break.

*Figure 5. The girls and Teresa in front of one of the rescue elephants. This particular elephant was known to be kind of a jerk.*

*Figure 6. Addison giving an elephant a pedicure. Each of the girls did a foot. I brushed the elephant with soap and water, and Teresa sprayed the elephant down with a hose.*

On the day we were to leave the KOA and head back up north, the final new experience was to expunge the accumulated waste water from the toilet system. By observing other RVs in the park, I needed to take the flushing hose (an expandable four-inch flexible hose) and put it down a drainpipe that was near the spigot by the parking spot (each parking spot had their own drain). The first step was to remove a cap from the bottom of the water control panel located in one of the cargo bays and attach the flushing hose, remembering to put the end of the hose in the drain. Once everything gets set up, a lever was pulled which opened a valve that allowed the black water tank (poop, pee, and toilet paper) to be emptied. Then a second lever was pulled that opened a second valve that allowed the gray water tank (water from the sinks) to be emptied. The order is important so that the gray water cleans out the flushing hose, hopefully washing away any residual black tank debris in the hose. The process seemed fairly simple. I spent a fair amount of time watching videos and reading the operating manual, so I was sure, since everything else had gone perfectly, that this would go in kind.

As I twisted open the cap, immediately the entire contents of the black tank came rushing out onto me, Winnie, and eventually the ground. I mumbled expletives. Nearly puked. Trying to get the cap back on, I got sprayed in the face with black water. Now there was a big f——cking mess on me, Winnie, and all over the ground. The plumbing cargo area had its own spray hose which I used to clean me, Winnie, and the ground near Winnie. More than anything, I did not want anyone to see what happened, so I tried to do this on the down-low, spraying the debris as far away from ground zero as possible. While it would have been nice to take a shower, I did not want to get caught having dumped a good amount of pee water plus toilet paper all over the ground, so I quickly got everything unhooked, raised the levelers, and got the hell out of there. I guess I am not as great as I thought. I would like to take the time now to publicly apologize to the Indianapolis KOA.

# HELPFUL HINT: YOU GOTTA JOIN

Assuming you plan to use your RV, I strongly recommend that you become a member of KOA, Good Sam Club, and Costco. Both KOA and Good Sam Club run RV parks. We stayed at a Good Sam Club park (Page, Arizona) but mostly stayed at KOAs. I joined Good Sam Club because membership gives you a discount on gas purchased at all Pilot Flying J locations. Pilot Flying Js are great places to stop because they have a great selection of food, and they usually have a dedicated RV refueling lane that reduces the possibility of destroying the pumps as you pull away—plus they have clean bathrooms. Getting the discount on gas is a bonus. The cost of a one-year membership is $29 and provides discounts on stays at Good Sam Club RV parks.

KOA membership also provides a discount on all stays at KOA parks. Since we stayed at KOA parks almost exclusively, I am much more familiar with KOAs. The cost of an annual KOA membership is $33. I can say that we more than covered our membership cost with the discounts we received from staying at KOA parks. I used their iPhone app to make almost every reservation. Both their online and app reservation systems are extremely easy to use. They include pictures of the facilities and descriptions (and pictures) of all amenities.

I love Costco. I love their products. I go there at least once a week. But when we had the RV, filling up the seventy-five-gallon gas tank was a kick in the nuts. A Costco membership means discounted gas, and the savings rack up. The challenge, of course, is finding a Costco as you travel. They may not be in a place you are going, but when you happen upon one, it is a great day.

# WELL...THAT NEEDS
# TO GET FIXED

T he first trip in Winnie was a success, until the disastrous end. Finding someone who could repair the plumbing system became a priority as I simply could not handle going through that again. Google helped find an RV repair shop in Elkhart, Indiana (home of the RV Hall of Fame and a number of RV manufacturers)—All Brand RV Repair Inc. Before I brought Winnie over for them, I needed to empty the black tank again. After dumping the tank contents on the ground at the Indianapolis KOA, I added more toilet treatment liquid to the toilet for the trip home. And as it turned out, it was a good idea because the bathroom was used on the way home from Indianapolis. This time, however, I was ready. I got elbow-length rubber gloves, a plastic bin, and a green trash bag. I put the bin below the cap in case there was some leakage from the garbage bag which I held over the cap. I slowly twisted the cap open, and out rushed the debris into the garbage bag. Yes, it smelled, but it was contained. Pulling the bag away, the few drops that remained fell into the plastic bin.

It took about a week or so for Winnie to get fixed. We had a deadline in that we wanted to tailgate with Winnie for the Notre Dame spring football game. After picking up Winnie, I thought, since I was in Elkhart (that is very RV centric), I would top off the propane tank. Using the furnace in Indianapolis had dropped the level to about half full, and I had seen a propane gas refill establishment that would be convenient to stop at on my way home. As I pulled into the complex, it looked like I needed to go through a gate to get to the office. As I made the turn to get past the gate, my brain farted, and I forgot I was driving a thirty-five-foot vehicle. As I made the turn, I heard the unmistakable sound of crunching wood. The gate had dug into the side of Winnie and was tearing a gash across her side. I was able to extricate Winnie from the talons of the gate, but the damage was done. To add insult to injury, when I went into the office to get the propane gas tank filled, I found out that I did not even need to get to the other side of the fence. They had a pump set up for RVs. Imagine every curse word you have ever heard or thought of. I yelled all of those on the way home. There was no one to blame. Strike that. There was only one person to blame, and that person was behind the f——cking wheel.

Upon getting home, I called my friends at All Brand RV Repair Inc. and asked them if they did body work.

ME: Hey, I just picked up an RV from you about twenty minutes ago. Do you do body work?

ALL BRAND: What could you possibly have done to your RV in twenty minutes?

ME: I tore it up going through a fence. Can you fix it?

ALL BRAND: Sure. [I did not hear this, but I assume they said after I hung up: What a f—cking moron].

My challenge at this point was to make sure we could tailgate at the spring football game with Winnie and make the gash seem less obvious. I did know that I had to keep moisture out. So I got a roll of white duct tape and covered up the gashes. Good news, Notre Dame won the game.

My biggest fear was what Teresa was going to say. I assumed she was going to be super turned on by my driving skilzzz.

ME: Hey, honey, guess what?

TERESA: What?

ME: I broke Winnie.

TERESA: What?

ME: Yep, tore a big gash in the side.

TERESA: Ha ha ha ha ha ha…

ME: You are probably not going to just forget this are you?

TERESA: Ha ha ha ha ha ha…(wiping a tear away). Hey, girls, guess what?

MY DAUGHTERS: What?

TERESA: Dad crashed Winni

MY DAUGHTERS: Ha ha ha ha ha…

ME: Ooof.

Winnie got repaired at a hefty cost of $1,400—an expensive brain fart.

# PLANNING A TRIP OF A LIFETIME

The original plan was to go out to Wyoming to dig for fossils. In the intervening time, my dinosaur-loving daughter had stopped loving dinosaurs. However, Teresa started doing some research on all the things we could see on our way out to dig for fossils. So our plan was to stop in the Badlands National Park, Mount Rushmore National Memorial, Custer State Park, Yellowstone National Park, Grand Teton National Park, fossil hunting, Pioneer days in Cheyenne, horse riding somewhere in Nebraska, a visit to my dad's cousin in Iowa, and then back home. At some point, and I am not sure how this was added, we decided the first leg of our trip was going to Saint Paul, Minneapolis, to visit some friends. I honestly really suck at logistics, and everyone in my family knows it.

FLASHBACK: Back in January 2011, we decided to take the girls to Disney World. The plan was for Teresa's parents to meet up with us so that we had extra hands to help with the girls as the twins were six and the youngest was four. As we were planning that trip, we could not find perfect times to travel on one airline, so we decided to make two one-way reservations. Teresa took care of the flights back and all of the hotel accommodations. My job was to book the flight to Orlando. I clearly recall finding the flights but, in hindsight, am a bit foggy on the paying for the flights. So we were to leave January 1 around 2:00 PM. I decided I would check in before dinner on December 31. I could not find the confirmation email from Expedia. I logged into Expedia only to find that I had reserved the flight but not paid for it. Alas, we needed to be in Orlando the next day and no way to get there. Thank God for Southwest Airlines. They had a flight leaving at 6:00 AM that had five seats available, and it only cost more than double what I was going to have to pay had I actually paid for the flights when I reserved them. The bonus of a 6:00 AM flight was that we got to wake up at 3:00 AM in order to have enough time to drive to Chicago to catch the flight. Happy New Year!

The planning for this trip started back in December 2015. I was paranoid that any RV park would be full when we needed to stay there. So given Teresa's required stops, our known summer schedule, and available vacation time, I set out a time line for the trip. The goal was to limit the driving time in any one day to eight hours. Once we sat down and went over the trip, I got approval to make the reservations at the RV parks. The itinerary for the trip was as follows:

- *Friday, July 15*: Granger, Indiana to Saint Paul, Minnesota (stayed on street in front of friend's house)—500 miles
- *Sunday, July 17*: Saint Paul, Minnesota, to the Badlands National Park (KOA near the Badlands)—540 miles
- *Monday, July 18*: the Badlands National Park to Mount Rushmore National Memorial (KOA near Mount Rushmore)—118 miles (via Wall Drug Store and Rapid City to pick up rental car)
- *Thursday, July 21*: Mount Rushmore National Park to Yellowstone National Park (one night in the park, two nights at KOA in West Yellowstone, Montana)—485 miles (via Rapid City to return rental car)
- *Sunday, July 24*: Yellowstone National Park to Grand Teton National Park (stayed in Colter Bay RV Park)—94 miles
- *Monday, July 25*: Grand Teton National Park to Rock Springs, Wyoming (KOA in Rock Springs, Wyoming)—233 miles
- *Tuesday, July 26*: Digging for fossils in the morning (Kemmerer, Wyoming), then Rock Springs, Wyoming, to Fort Collins, Colorado (KOA in Fort Collins, Colorado)—459 miles

- *Thursday, July 28*: Fort Collins, Colorado, to Lincoln, Nebraska (KOA in Lincoln, Nebraska)—519 miles
- *Friday, July 29*: Lincoln, Nebraska, to Quad Cities, Illinois (KOA in Rock Island, Illinois)—326 miles
- *Saturday, July 30*: Quad Cities, Illinois, to Granger, Indiana (home)—249 miles

If you are counting, that is an expected drive of 3,523 miles.

# HELPFUL HINT: PLAN AHEAD

I do not want to sound paranoid, but the more complex the trip, the earlier you want to plan all of the stops. RV parks fill up which is going to leave you out of luck if you wait to the last minute, especially if you are traveling to a place where lots of people want to go. We reserved all of the RV park stays over six months ahead of time. Many national parks require you to make reservations at least a year in advance. The early planning allowed us to find a spot that had all the amenities we needed (hookups for electricity and water and a tank dump station at the parking spot) for the size RV we were driving. Note that the RV park in Yellowstone National Park had size limits, and we just barely fit. The websites and phone apps allow you to take care of this quite easily (though most of my experience was with KOA sites and the KOA app). The KOA sites usually allow you to cancel reservations if your plans change, but there is a limitation on the time frame where a refund will be provided.

# DRESS REHEARSAL BEFORE
# THE BIG SHOW

Having learned some valuable lessons with our trip to Indianapolis, we decided to take Winnie on a longer drive to test her out, again. This time, we took her to our annual trip to Ocean City, Maryland. Normally we would stop at my parents' house in Potomac, Maryland, on the way there, but this time we were going to push all the way there. Overall, the trip was 727 miles and should take around twelve hours if traveling by car. This was going to be the first time we drove in summer conditions, so I was curious how that was going to work out.

We were much more comfortable getting Winnie ready for the trip. There seemed to be a bit of an issue with the house batteries, so I decided to replace them. They did not seem to be charging properly, meaning anything in the RV that needed electricity as we drove was not going to work without the house batteries, including the generator (and thus the coach air conditioner). I took the old ones out and brought them to a Batteries Plus where I was able to purchase a duplicate size of battery. I installed the new house batteries, and we were good to go. The generator cranked right up, and all was good.

Because of limited vacation time from work, Teresa was going to work for a few days then fly to join us in Ocean City. As such, it was me and the girls on a long journey together. While the trip was long, there were no real challenges, except it seemed that the electrical system had drained the house batteries again. We knew the house batteries were low because the RV let out an ear-piercing beep. Think of the sound your smoke detector makes when it has a low battery, then turn up the volume to eleven. I thought that the batteries would be charged by the alternator system. It seemed dumb that the house batteries would drain so quickly, especially since they were new batteries. I read all I could about the electrical system in the manual, but it provided zero information for this scenario. Nothing about the beep. Nothing about the batteries recharging. The internet suggested I check all of the fuses. I checked the fuses I could find, and nothing seemed out of the ordinary. Finally, I had to suck up my pride and call Matt (the RV guru who had given us the one-and-a-half-hour tutorial on Winnie). The first thing he had me do was check the fuse box under the dashboard.

MATT: Check the fuse box under the dashboard.
ME: Okay. How do I do that?
MATT: Go to the dashboard and lift it up.
ME: It lifts up?
MATT: Yes.
ME: Which fuse should I check?
MATT: Look at the diagram that is attached under the dashboard.
ME: There is a diagram?
MATT: Yes.
ME: Oh, look. The fuse for the side-view mirror is burned out. That is why it is not working. All the others seem fine.
MATT: Look at the circuit breakers under the stairs.
ME: There are circuit breakers under the stairs?
MATT: Yes.
ME: Oooooh. Look. There is a button sticking out.
MATT: Push it in.
ME: Okay.
MATT: The house batteries will now charge.
ME: You are an RV Jedi.
MATT: Yes.

Note that all of Matt's instructions came from memory. There was no FaceTime or any other visual aid. He just knows RVs. Like all RVs. He is an RV savant. By the way, there is a very good chance when I was fixing the side mirror I broke going through the toll booth, when I cut the wires I not only blew the fuse for the side mirror but also caused this particular circuit breaker to trip.

There was one other issue that came up with our trip. The air-conditioning from the front console was not working. I thought it might just be a Freon issue, but I did a bit of googling and found that some RVers run the generator to run the house air conditioner while driving. So my plan was to do that on the way home. To do that, I needed the house batteries to charge. I plugged the RV into my parent's beach house, and it seemed to help charge the house batteries. I could see the charge on those batteries increasing.

There was some road construction on the Pennsylvania Turnpike on the way to the beach, so I had asked some friends about alternative routes. And they suggested taking a different highway through western Maryland to get to Pittsburgh. As it turned out, that highway (US 68) went through the Appalachian mountain range just like the Pennsylvania Turnpike, but it had much steeper inclines. Poor Winnie. I heard noises coming from the engine I had never heard before. It sounded like something was winding up, and it scared me because if something goes wrong with the engine, I am screwed. I have no idea how to fix that. Plus, as we were careening down one of the mountains, the check brakes light came on. It eventually went out, so I did not think much about it.

In addition, as it turned out, road construction in Pennsylvania was not isolated to the Pennsylvania toll road. In fact, the amount of road construction projects we went through was significantly higher, and the speeds we drove were significantly slower than had we just taken the toll road. What was supposed to take twelve hours took us eighteen.

When we got back, I called my friends at All Brand RV Repair Inc. and asked if they worked on air conditioners, and they said they did not. However, they knew of a business (Merrill and Robichaud Automotive) that did, so I took Winnie over to them to look at the air conditioner. Our trip was a month away, and I assumed that there would be no issue getting an air conditioner fixed in a few weeks.

When I dropped Winnie off, they asked me to park her in their fenced-in back lot. Oh, God, another fence. Needless to say, I took it slow. I drove Winnie through that fence like Rainman drove his dad's car around the driveway—slow and steady. After a week, I called and no movement on the air conditioner. After two weeks, I called, and they were still working on it. Finally, a few days before we were to leave, they said they had been able to get the air conditioner working, sort of. At that point, I would have taken anything. They also gave Winnie a once-over to make sure she was good for the trip, and before I left, they made sure all the tires had the right air pressure. They said there were some issues with the air conditioner they simply could not figure out, though I am sure they did not even come close to charging me for the time they spent looking. Winnie had some air-conditioning coming from the front dashboard, as long as I did not put the AC on high.

The next week was all about getting packed and preparing Winnie for the trip. She was fueled up and charged up, and so were we.

# HELPFUL HINT: THE BATTERIES

This description of the house batteries would have been helpful for the previous section Winnie had three batteries: one for the engine and two to run electronics in the cabin (called the house batteries). The engine battery is no different from the battery you have in your car and is designed to provide a burst of current for starting the engine. House batteries are deep-cycle batteries that are designed to provide a steady amount of current over a longer period of time. There are options on the house batteries setup. My first set of replacements were exactly like the ones that Winnie had when we purchased her: two twelve-volt deep-cycle batteries wired in parallel.

When winterizing the RV in cold climates, removing the batteries is really important. If the water in the batteries freezes, the battery may be ruined and might split. I know this from experience. The second time I replaced the house batteries I chose to use two six-volt golf cart batteries (also deep-cycle batteries) wired in series which then provided the twelve volts necessary. A number of websites recommended this setup.

It is also worth purchasing a battery charger or two. I purchased two that allowed me to get the house batteries and starter battery fully charged before we used Winnie, which made a big difference on being able to use some of the electronics (lights, charging electronics, etc.) in the cabin. I bought one on Amazon (NOCO Genius G3500 6V/12V 3.5A UltraSafe Smart Battery Charger) and a second one at Walmart (VIP 70W Fully Automatic Battery Charger, 6V/12V Lead-Acid Auto Battery Charger/Maintainer w/ LCD Digital Display). Both worked great and charged all three batteries without any problems.

# HELPFUL HINT: TOOLS AND THINGS YOU MIGHT WANT TO BRING

**W**hile I am not a mechanic and do not pretend to be, there are some tools that we found very helpful to have for the trip:

- A full set of socket wrenches
- A full set of screw drivers
- Hammer
- An electric impact driver
- Wire cutters
- Wire strippers
- Duct tape
- Wire tape
- Drill (though an impact driver can act as a drill with the right kind of bits)
- Drill bits
- A full set of pliers including needle-nose pliers and locking pliers
- A long extension cord (150 feet) is useful not only to plug in power tools but also to connect with a shore line (term used to refer to plugging in the RV to power) at a non-RV park (RV park shore lines are located next to the RV and will accept 120-volt, 30-ampere or 50-ampere connections).

I recommend bringing some hardware such as the following:

- Washers of different sizes
- Self-drilling screws (of different sizes—I prefer GRK, sold at Home Depot)
- Wire connectors (I prefer the port style to the crimp or screw on connectors)
- A tube of liquid nails
- A tube of silicone sealant

Having a vacuum cleaner can help keep the cabin tidy, as crumbs tend to build up on a long trip, or clean up when a box of cereal spills on the floor. We also bought a portable gas grill so that we could grill hamburgers, hot dogs, chicken, steak, etc. It used the green portable gas containers that you can get at any grocery store or Walmart, and we brought a couple extra gas containers just in case.

I also recommend bringing a six-foot-long two-by-four and at least four- to eight-foot-long pieces of two-by-eight. The two-by-four was a recommendation from Matt (the RV guru) to use in case the levelers do not go up all the way. You can use this to manually push them up (use it as a lever). The two-by-eight pieces are to be used under the levelers. Many RV parks require pads under the levelers. Also, if your parking space is particularly nonlevel, it will provide additional height to get the RV level.

I also recommend having extra front headlights in case one goes out. Our RV lights were not particularly bright, so when one went out, it was difficult to see at night. I was lucky that a local Ocean City AutoZone happen to have the right size of bulb. I also recommend getting extra taillight bulbs and to upgrade the taillight bulbs to LED. You can get them on Amazon. Also, get extra fuses. You can get a multipack of automotive fuses with a fuse tester and puller for about $20 at Home Depot or through Amazon. An extra set of windshield wipers is useful. At the very least, make sure the windshield wipers are good and in working condition. Further, get windshield cleaner (I found Invisible Glass does the best job). There will be lots of bug splatter on your windshield. If you are driving west as the sun sets, the bug splatter will make it very difficult to see. Make sure to fill the windshield cleaner fluid and bring a container of refill. They have lots of options on windshield cleaner fluid, and I recommend one that helps get the bug grime off and repels rain.

As for paper products, make sure you have the right kind of toilet paper. There is specific RV/boat rapid dissolving toilet paper which should be used. Never use normal toilet paper, it will clog the system. Purchase lots of toilet treatment to make sure the toilet does not stink. Bring lots of paper towels as well. These come in handy for spills as well as cleaning the windshield. If you can fit it in, a small stepping stool helps to clean the windshield. I did not have one and had to improvise to be able to clean the windshield every morning before we drove off.

# HELPFUL HINT: MAKE THE BEDS MORE COMFORTABLE

**W**innie had three sleeping areas: bedroom, pullout couch, and the kitchen table area. The beds were really not that comfortable to sleep on. To make the sleeping arrangements more comfortable for us, I purchased memory foam mattress toppers for all sleeping areas. Each bed area was the size of a queen bed, and I went with a three-inch-deep mattress topper. This was an awesome decision. No one complained, except at each stop two of our daughters had to share a bed. After the big trip out west, I purchased a Sleep and Store Constant Comfort Inflatable EZ Bed (twin-size) so that each of our daughters could sleep in their own bed. When Winnie's slide-out was extended, this inflatable bed fit perfectly next to the kitchen table bed, allowing a pathway to get past it to the bathroom. I got a twin mattress topper for this bed as well. Peace came to the family.

To store the mattress toppers while driving, we put them all on top of the bedroom mattress. This made that bed the ultimate comfort lounger as there was a foot of memory foam to lie on.

# AND AWAY WE GO—GRANGER, INDIANA, TO SAINT PAUL, MINNESOTA

**T**he day we were to leave on our trip was full of excitement and last-minute preparations. We could not leave until Teresa got home from work, usually around 2:30 PM. From clothes, food, snacks, tools, pillows, blankets, gas, etc., we were ready to go. Our dogs and house were going to be cared for by a dog/house sitter. We finally pulled out of the driveway around 3:00 PM, hoping to beat the Friday rush hour traffic in Chicago. Once we hit the Indiana Toll Road, I immediately regretted not looking at Google Maps or Waze because the toll road was jacked up with traffic. All summer, they had been working on rebuilding the bridges and repaving the surface of the toll road. What should have been an hour to get out of Indiana took two. And as luck would have it, we landed in the Friday Chicago rush hour traffic just in time for it to take an additional hour to get past Chicago. I relied on Waze to guide me past Chicago, which I believe was a complete mistake. What I should have done is take a little bit of time to figure out the best route to get around Chicago, even if it had taken us a few more miles out of our way. I was putting 100 percent trust that Waze and/or Google Maps was going to do me right. This was something I would regret over and over and over.

The traffic finally lightened up around Rockford, Illinois, and the plan was to stop for dinner somewhere near Madison, Wisconsin. We would need to fill up with gas around there, so it seemed like the best option. I think I had seen a billboard for a mall, so I suggested that might be an easy place to find a parking space. We decided the mall food court would work in that everyone could find something they might want to eat, as our daughters can be a bit picky with food. With everyone fueled up, including Winnie, we set off to Saint Paul. We fueled up once more before reaching Saint Paul. I called our friend to let them know we were approaching, where he gave absurdly detailed instructions to get to his house. I said "sure, sure" and simply did what Waze told me to do. We arrived around midnight.

The neighborhoods in Saint Paul were not well designed for a thirty-five-foot RV, but we were able to make it to their house where their neighbor allowed us to park in front of their house and plug Winnie in. They were RV people, so they understood. After showing them Winnie, I mentioned that this was the only trip we were taking with Winnie, and she was for sale as soon as we got back. They made what appeared to be a reasonable offer to purchase Winnie, so that night, I was pretty sure we were soon going to be former RV owners. We stayed the night in Winnie. There was a big thunderstorm which freaked our girls out, but once it passed, the weather was cool so we could open the windows. One night down, and all was well.

We spent the next day exploring the Saint Paul, Minneapolis, area with our friends. We saw the Mississippi River and Minnehaha Falls and attended a street fair near their house. We ended the day at our friend's brother's house. Not only did they have a pool, but they also had kids our girls could play with. It was a super casual Saturday and helped us mentally prepare for the next day's drive to the Badlands National Park.

*Figure 7. The family at Minnehaha Falls.*

# HELPFUL HINT: GO WHEN YOUR KIDS ARE IN THE FOURTH GRADE

**T**he National Park Service has a program where kids in the fourth grade and their families get into all national parks for free. This may seem trivial, but it can save quite a bit of money. National parks charge somewhere between $5 and $40 to get in (some charge by vehicle, and some by person) but not if you have a fourth grader and you have filled out the form online. The nice national park ranger at the gate will ask a question or two of the fourth grader, and off you go. At the first park you enter, you will exchange your paper pass for a plastic card with the kid's name on it. If you are one who puts together keepsakes, it is worth keeping. We are not. To get your pass, google "national parks fourth-grade pass" or try this website: https://www.nationalparks.org/our-work/campaigns-initiatives/every-kid-outdoors

# SAINT PAUL TO THE BADLANDS NATIONAL PARK

I have to admit that when my wife suggested we stop at the Badlands (a place I had never heard of in over fifty years of life), I thought she was off her rocker. In any event, from Teresa's research, it was a place you cannot skip. When we headed off early on a Sunday morning, I was not exactly excited about the final destination. In fact, it seemed like this drive was going to be long and boring, and I was trying to remember why we had driven so far north to Saint Paul in the first place. Perhaps it was karma because we not only got to spend a day with great friends but also I may have found someone to buy Winnie. Escaping Saint Paul early on Sunday morning was simple. We headed down south via Interstate 35 to Interstate 90, heading west. It was a bit windy, which made driving Winnie a bit like sailing, but I was able to keep her straight. South Minnesota does not have a lot of visual appeal. I am sure the people are nice.

Driving with little to see, you notice billboards. We started to see billboards for the Corn Palace in Mitchell, South Dakota. When my wife suggested we stop, I was less than supportive.

TERESA: We should stop at the Corn Palace.
ME: The what?
TERESA: The Corn Palace.
ME: The what?
TERESA: The Corn Palace. It is in Mitchell, South Dakota. Have you not seen the billboards?

ME: Yea, but why go there?

TERESA: What else are we going to do? You have plans? We will have
been in this damn rolling box for five hours. We need to get
out." (This may not have been her exact words, but this was
what I heard. One hundred percent sure she was much nicer
but disappointed in my bad attitude. She would have many
more disappointments ahead.)

ME: Fine. Let me know how to get there (sulking).

TERESA: It will be a fun adventure.

ME: What a waste of time (not audible).

So we pulled off Interstate 90 at Mitchell, South Dakota. The
Corn Palace was a few miles off the interstate. The parking lot was
huge. I had no idea that this was such a big deal. Upon walking up
to the Corn Palace, I was amazed. The entire outside of the building
was made of corn of different colors. There were murals all made out
of different colored corn. We went into the Corn Palace, and there
were tractors to climb on and information about the history of corn
and the Corn Palace. And, of course, there was a gift shop where we
purchased a Corn Palace Christmas ornament. We then went across
the street and had some ice cream and sat outside for a few minutes.
I was really glad we stopped at the Corn Palace. This really reinforced
to everyone that my instincts suck, and I can be kind of a shithead.

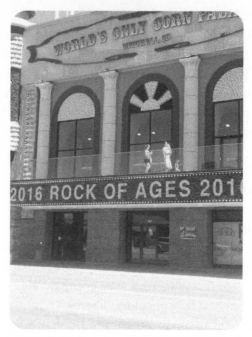

*Figure 8. Outside of the Corn Palace, Mitchell, South Dakota.*

*Figure 9. The girls on a tractor inside the Corn Palace.*

*Figure 10. Mural on the side of the Corn Palace.*

Three hours later, we pulled up to the Badlands National Park. You go from flat Midwest cornfields to Mars. I remember as we were pulling up, my jaw was agape. I could not believe what I was seeing. My daughters, who had spent much of the day staring at screens, suddenly stopped. They were speechless staring out the windows of Winnie as we approached this indescribable landscape. The jagged hills were shaded pink, purple, and white. This was the first time I was going to take Winnie through a park entrance, and I had no idea what to expect.[2] Because my twin daughters had just finished fourth grade, they qualified us all to enter all national parks for free, but I had no idea how this was supposed to work. I handed the ranger a pass I had printed out, and he called Lily up to the front. He asked her how old she was and what grade she was in. He then gave us a

---

[2] My only experience with park rangers before this point was when I was in high school, and a bunch of us had gone to Great Falls National Park in Maryland where a park ranger kicked me out for bringing beer.

plastic pass with her name we could use at all national parks. He did not even ask what was in our cooler.

*Figure 11. The girls looking out Winnie's windows as we entered the Badlands National Park.*

We meandered through the park to the KOA campground just outside of the park. Teresa's mother had traveled with a friend to meet us. We hooked Winnie up, and the girls went for a dip in the KOA swimming pool. After dinner, we drove back into the park (I do not recall if we unhooked Winnie or if we crammed into my mother-in-law's car) for an evening program sponsored by the Park Service on star gazing and to climb on the hills surrounding the park information center. The good news was that, as tired as we were given the extremely long day, when we got back and were getting ready to sleep, the girls decided that was the time to argue about who was sleeping in what bed and who had to double up. Good times.

# EXPLORING THE BADLANDS AND THE JUNIOR RANGER PROGRAM

**W**e woke up, cooked everyone breakfast (pancakes), dumped the tanks (no problems), unhooked, and headed for a few hours of exploring the Badlands National Park. The first stop was the Park Information Center to get a map of the park. I am uncertain how it happened, but before we could go about our business of exploring, each of my daughters had a Junior Ranger booklet which they needed to complete. In exchange for completing the booklet they would get a Junior Ranger badge. About 45 minutes later, we had wrapped up the Junior Ranger booklet. At the time, I was cursing the existence of this process. We had to go to all of the exhibits at the information center to find answers to questions. There were puzzles, find-the-word games, etc. Addison decided early on in the process she had no interest in a badge or becoming a junior ranger. Lily and Kelsey were determined to complete the booklet and get the badge. Finally, with the help of me, my wife, and the Internet, we finished and turned in the booklet. In exchange, the girls were sworn in as junior rangers and received their small plastic/wooden badges.

*Figure 12. Badlands Junior Ranger badge.*

At some point, as we were trying to complete this booklet, my daughters saw another girl with a green Junior Ranger vest replete with dozens of these Junior Ranger badges. Their eyes bugged out with excitement with the prospect that they could earn dozens of badges and maybe get a vest. I just thought to myself, *Please let this be the last time I have to do this.* There was way too much stress in completing these booklets. However, as it turned out, thanks to working on the booklets, we all learned quite a bit about the park and its fauna and flora—something we would never have learned without the booklet. With some distance and perspective, I am really glad we spent the time.

We spent the next couple of hours stopping at various parts of the park to climb on the rocks and see what there was to see. Finally, we began the journey to Wall Drug Store in Wall, South Dakota. Driving through South Dakota, I think we saw hundreds of signs stating we had to stop. So we did. It is hard to describe, but it is certainly a unique place to stop. We ate lunch and did some shopping.

We purchased several sets of binoculars, so we did not need to fight over who got to use the one set we had. We had some ice cream, then set off for Mount Rushmore.

*Figure 13. The family exploring the Badlands National Park.*

*Figure 14. The girls at the Badlands.*

*Figure 15. The family outside of Wall Drug.*

# RAPID CITY, THEN MOUNT RUSHMORE—YOU SUCK, GOOGLE AND WAZE

**W**e had to stop in Rapid City to pick up a rental car for the few days we were going to be at Mount Rushmore. I think it is safe to say that I was underprepared and undertrained to drive Winnie. I could not imagine what a shit show it would have been had I tried to tow a car behind us. To eliminate that need, I reserved a rental car at all of the stops where I believed we would need one. After completing the paperwork for the rental car, we were off to the Mount Rushmore KOA, Teresa driving the rental car and me driving Winnie. I was paranoid about the route we should take to get to the KOA as it appeared on the map that there were two options, and I had no idea which was better. There was a fork in the road, and you have to decide to go right or left. I decided to solicit the help of Google Maps and Waze. I had them both verbally giving me directions so I did not screw this up. When I got to the fork where Highway 16 splits to Highway 16 and 16A, both Google Maps and Waze told me to go right (stay on Highway 16). For some reason, my wife's map app told her to go left at the fork (and go on Highway 16A). In any event, I listened to both of my map programs, presumably programmed by intelligent people, guided by GPS, to guide me safely to my intended destination. At some point, both apps were telling me to turn left. I was on a four-lane highway with what appeared to be woods on the left, but I did what they told me to do. The left, however, was onto a one-lane dirt road. Now I was f——cked. I could not turn around. I could not back up onto a highway.

I stopped and got out of Winnie to discuss my options with my wife. She told me I should have gone left at the fork. Not really helpful as I had two apps telling me to go right at the fork and then turn left onto this one-lane dirt road. Given I had no real other option, we decided to continue forward. If possible, I might be able to find a spot to turn around. After several miles of one-lane dirt road, the road got a bit wider and was gravel. After a few miles of that, there seemed to be some man-made things indicating that humans actually could travel here. Finally, we ended up at the back entrance of the KOA. No idea how that happened. Winnie was covered in dust and dirt. As we drove through the KOA on our way to the office, I asked for directions.

ME: Excuse me (to a KOA employee after I rolled down the window), which way to the office?

KOA EMPLOYEE: You just come through the service entrance?

ME: I guess. Google told me to do that.

KOA EMPLOYEE: Yep, sometimes that happens to some people (kind of chuckling at me).

ME: Kinda dodgy.

KOA EMPLOYEE: Yep.

Once properly oriented, I realized what an amazingly nice place this was. There were waterslides, restaurants, horse rentals, pools, swing sets, etc. This was going to be great. Our plans were to visit Mount Rushmore that evening after dinner for their lighting ceremony. But first, we were going to enjoy all the stuff this KOA had to offer. We spent some time at the pools, waterslides, and swing set. Before dinner, we decided to take a shower (at the KOA shower rooms). While I was starting dinner, a thunderstorm blew up. I had finished cooking chicken breasts on the grill and was finalizing the side dishes. Meanwhile, my wife was in the shower room when the thunderstorm took a nasty twist, and it started hailing, really hard. My wife was trapped in the shower room, and I was in Winnie with

the girls (and my mother-in-law). Poor Winnie was getting pummeled with hail, and I was thinking that the hail could break something on Winnie's roof. At least the girls were freaking out. That
made it better.

# VISITING MOUNT RUSHMORE—BUCKET LIST

I never thought I would be able to see Mount Rushmore in person. I could not envision ever being in South Dakota. The fact that we were a mere six miles away brought a heightened level of excitement to my spirit. Once the rain had passed and we had eaten dinner, we packed into our rental car for a short drive over to Mount Rushmore National Memorial. There was a lighting ceremony that evening where they were going to light up the faces on Mount Rushmore. Turning into the driveway to get to the parking garage at Mount Rushmore National Memorial, you look straight at the iconic sight of the four presidents. It actually took my breath away. I think I exclaimed "that's it!"

*Figure 16. Kelsey picking George Washington's nose. Always funny.*

*Figure 17. The girls at the base of Mount Rushmore.*

Before the ceremony, we walked around the grounds where you can get up close to the mountain and get some awesome views. The pathway takes you to the studio of Gutzon Borglum, the sculptor of Mount Rushmore, where you can see a small model of the sculpture (through a window). There is a chance that you might get to go inside the studio during the day or get a guided tour by a park ranger, but we were there fairly late in the evening. We made our way over to the amphitheater area facing the mountain where the Park Service had a program scheduled. Unfortunately, the video system was not working due to the storm that had dropped the hail earlier. So the park ranger did her part to explain the history of the sculpture and the artist in lieu of the video that they were hoping to show. Near the end of the program, all members of the military (past and present) in attendance were invited on stage. The park ranger took the time to have each person tell the crowd their name, service, and unit. There may have been over fifty service members on stage. Each received a nice ovation. When that was done, there was a flag-lowering cere-mony. Then they turned on the lights illuminating the four faces of Mount Rushmore. Everyone walked away happy.

# EXPERIENCING KEYSTONE, SOUTH DAKOTA

I realize I should keep to our driving experience, but it is worth noting that there are other things to do near Mount Rushmore besides just seeing stone faces. Just down the road from Mount Rushmore is Keystone, South Dakota. This town has a few restaurants and bars. It also has an area that includes an alpine slide, ropes course, and zip lines. We decided to go to Rushmore Tramway Adventures for the morning. My mother-in-law joined us as I talked trash about how she would be riding the alpine slide like an old lady and how I did not want to go behind her as she was going to hold everyone up. We did the ropes course first, which was sufficiently challenging for everyone, though one of my daughters felt sick and bailed out. I have a feeling she was dehydrated as it was very dry and hot. Afterward, we did the zip line then took a chairlift to the top of the hill where there was a restaurant and the starting line for the alpine slide. After lunch, we headed for the alpine slide. Everyone was old enough to ride by themselves, but our youngest chose to ride with me. What I really recall was my mother-in-law kicking my ass in getting down the alpine slide. There were two tracks side by side, and each car had a brake. My mother-in-law beating me down the mountain was caused either by me having Kelsey riding with me or I was just a colossal puss, perhaps both.

*Figure 18. Me and Kelsey at the ropes course in Keystone, South Dakota.*

*Figure 19. Addison, Ella (my mother-in-law),*
*and Lily at the top of the alpine slide.*

*Figure 20. Teresa added to Mount Rushmore.*

On the advice of my brother, we decided to venture to Bear Country USA. This is a drive-through park where you can see bears and other wildlife up close. You can also park and walk around in part of the attraction. Not too far from Bear Country USA was a Walmart where we loaded up on essentials for the next leg of our trip.

*Figure 21. Baby black bear climbing a tree at Bear Country USA.*

# CUSTER STATE PARK AND CRAZY HORSE MEMORIAL

Our final day at the Mount Rushmore area, we wanted to see bison. There was apparently a large herd of bison at Custer State Park in Custer, South Dakota. There were two routes from the Mount Rushmore KOA to get to Custer State Park: a shorter way and a longer way. My assumption was that we were going to take the shorter route. I let Teresa lead us, but as I had discovered, she was okay with driving off grid[3]. Further, two of my daughters get carsick, so I try to avoid routes that have lots of turns through mountain passes. In hindsight, nobody puked in the car, so no harm no foul. However, at the time, not knowing where we were going and

---

[3] FLASHBACK: A year earlier (pre-Winnie), we decided to visit Mammoth Cave National Park, home of the largest set of caverns in the world. Teresa was copilot and providing me directions. At some point, we turned off the interstate, which I assume means we were close to our intended destination. As it turned out, no. We were traversing through very rural Kentucky. At one point, I saw a sign that read Road Ends in Water. I hesitated for a minute to contemplate the sign, then asked my wife if she saw the sign, which she did and was equally confused. What could it mean that the road ends in water? Again, we saw the sign further down the road. Now I started getting worried. Eventually, the road started to descend down, and sure enough, the road ended into a river. But there was a one-car ferry that would bring you across. As we were waiting for the ferry, I asked why we were going this way as it could not have been the fastest route. My wife said it was not, but she thought it might be nice to be off the interstate. Though she often gets me to where I want to go, I learned to rely on Waze or Google Maps to bring me where I need to go. Of course, all bets are off when you have no cell service.

no cell service to guide us, I was a bit confused why we were taking the scenic route. The highlight was turning the corner and seeing, through a tunnel, Mount Rushmore perfectly framed (this is called the Iron Mountain Road). There was also a pigtail bridge, which was a 360-degree loop bridge. Meandering through the woods got a bit uncomfortable, especially at one point when we came upon a fork in the road and had to make blindly a right/left decision. Surprisingly, we guessed correctly (stay on Highway 16A, so take a right).

Pulling into the state park was a bit disappointing as we had to pay $20 to enter (they do not accept fourth-grade National Park Service passes). In the visitor center, they had a program similar to Junior Rangers, but the girls decided they did not want to participate as it did not yield a fancy badge. We watched some short videos and got the 411 on where the bison herds were. Driving through Custer State Park, I did not see shit. At one point, we saw a sightseeing jeep pull of the road and head over a hill. My wife made me pull over so she could walk out into the abyss to see what was over the hill. She coaxed Kelsey to follow, while my other two daughters and I sat in the car, judging how irresponsible it was to wander out into the wild. Did I mention the temperature was in the nineties? Soon a park ranger pulled off and approached Teresa and Kelsey to tell them how dangerous it was to do what they had done (not just because of the bison but also because of the danger of rattlesnakes). I felt vindicated. My wife was dismissive of the warnings from the park ranger as she told us how cool it was to look over the crest of the hill to see a large herd of bison.

*Figure 22. Bison my wife saw when she and Kelsey went off.*

As we ventured forth, I continued to see no wildlife. Total bust. We did happen upon a herd of feral burros who had been tamed from visitors feeding them. We pet the burros, then instantly regretted it because they kind of smelled (okay, I regretted petting the burros, and no one else in the car seemed to care).

*Figure 23. Addison and Kelsey petting one of the burros.*

As we neared the exit to Custer State Park, I declared an epic failure on the bison viewing, until we found ourselves trapped within a herd on either side of the road. They blindly crossed in front of cars, not giving a shit, knowing those pussies in the cars were going to stop. And stop we did. There were a couple of bison smashing each other in the head, grunting, and chasing each other around, presumably over a girl. Boys are dumb.

*Figure 24. Bison crossing in front of our car near the exit to Custer State Park.*

Once clear of the bison herd, we were off to the Crazy Horse Memorial. Think of it as Mount Rushmore in progress but bigger. The sculpture they are making includes Crazy Horse pointing while riding a horse. But they are transforming a granite mountain. To gain entrance to the Crazy Horse Memorial costs $30 per car, but it is worth it to help fund this amazing project. I am going to skip the details of the experience because I do not want to come off as preachy, but I strongly recommend reading about the memorial, its history, and the people building it. After watching a video on the history of the memorial, watching some Native American dancing, and having lunch at the restaurant, we purchased some chunks of granite[4] and headed back to Winnie.

---

[4]  Buying chunks of granite reminds me of Mardi Gras. I lived in the New Orleans area for seven years. If you had asked me before moving there (or since leaving) if I cared about a plastic necklace, I would think you daft. However, in the moment of a Mardi Gras parade (or any night on Bourbon Street), that plastic necklace is the most important thing on earth. In the moment of being at the Crazy Horse Memorial, buying chunks of granite seemed so important, but in the sobriety of time passing, it is just three chucks of granite that live in my garage.

*Figure 25. The mountain sculpture is behind this rendition of
what the mountain will look like once the sculpture is done.*

Getting back to the Mount Rushmore KOA, we went back to
the pool and waterslides. In addition, I took my hand at panning
for gold. You could buy a bag of sand that had some gold flakes
mixed in, along with a gold pan. Having watched *Gold Rush* on the
Discovery Channel since its inception (it should be called "winter
is coming and the equipment has broken down"), I was sure I had
become a gold mining expert. I spent the better part of an hour and a
half meticulously panning for gold. I believed I found the gold flakes
and put them in the small vile that came with the sand and gold pan.
Neither my wife nor my daughters believed I had gold in the vile.
The hell with them, I had gold in that damn vile.

*Figure 26. My vile with gold flakes. Haters are gonna hate.*

# THE DRIVING DAY
# I FEARED THE MOST

**B**ack in the planning stages of the trip, the longest drive was going to be between Mount Rushmore and Yellowstone National Park. The plan was to get up at the ass crack of dawn, drop off the rental car in Rapid City, and then head west into the mountains. Unlike the other trips, there was a specific time we had to be at our final destination. We were staying at the RV park inside of Yellowstone for the first night and needed to be there before 8:00 PM. If we left at 5:00 AM, I figured that we would have no trouble getting to Yellowstone by 5:00 or 6:00 PM. My biggest concern was a mountain range we had to drive through. The interstate went north and around all of the steep inclines of the various mountain ranges but added at least two hours to the trip if we chose to go the safe route. We did not. I spent quite a bit of time on the Internet, researching whether it would be safe driving an RV through the Bighorn National Forest and the Bighorn Mountain Range. I looked at the roads on Google Earth. In the end, it seemed something that Winnie would be able to handle.

Shortly after getting on the interstate near Rapid City, Teresa informed me that we were driving close to Devils Tower, and she wanted to stop. I panicked inside as this was going to eat into any time flexibility we might have but decided to go for it since I did not expect I would be coming this way again. I had always wondered about Devils Tower since seeing Richard Dreyfuss go batshit crazy in *Close Encounters of the Third Kind* when I was a kid. Once near Devils

Tower, we roused the kids out of their beds, ate a quick breakfast, and ventured out to experience Devils Tower, quickly (I hoped). A quick viewing was immediately quashed when my daughters discovered they could get another Junior Ranger badge. To get the badge required a walk around Devils Tower and full immersion into the visitor center. Two hours later, we were back on the road, and my asshole was even more puckered because we were now on a very tight schedule.

*Figure 27. As we approached Devils Tower, we woke the girls up for a picture with Devils Tower in the background.*

*Figure 28. The girls as we traversed Devils Tower.*

*Figure 29. Devils Tower Junior Ranger badge.*

The big decision point was turning off the interstate at Buffalo, Wyoming. We filled up with gas, we each got a snack at the convenience store, and I grew a pair of balls as we were at the point of no return. The choice was either to head forth into the mountains or go back to the interstate. We chose to enter the unknown of the Bighorn Mountains. I had downloaded an altimeter so that I could keep track of the altitude, for shits and giggles. Winnie had never been at high altitude, but that was about to change. Lucky for us, there was very little traffic on Highway 16. The road was well maintained, and there seemed to be a passing lane at most steep inclines, which were many. We kept going up, then down a little, then up a lot. Winnie was struggling. Full accelerator was going up the hills, and we were barely going thirty-five miles per hour. Then a horrible noise kicked in. That same noise we heard coming home from Ocean City the stupid way. Winnie's engine was getting hot, and the air was getting thin. We passed nine thousand feet above sea level with Winnie wheezing. At some point, I had a thought: *Going up really sucks, but how much is it going to suck going down?"* We finally reached what seemed like the top of the mountain when I saw a sign: Caution: Steep Grade Decline Next 12 Miles. *Oh, shit,* I thought to myself.

I tried to keep Winnie under control on our descent, but it was hard. She would build up lots of momentum, and I was ill equipped to deal with this. I really did not want to careen off the side of the mountain, so I was relying on the brakes. At some point, I had this conversation:

LILY: Dad, what smells like it is burning?
ME: WHAT?
LILY: It smells like something is burning.
ME: F———ck (quietly)!

I looked out the side mirror to see that smoke was coming out from under Winnie. I pulled over as soon as I had a place to pull over. We were in the middle of the Tensleep Canyon, but my concern was not the beauty around me but the smoke coming from the brakes. I had no idea what to do.

*Figure 30. Panoramic view of Tensleep Canyon. You can see a corner of Winnie's shadow to the left.*

My wife did what she had become all too familiar with: getting out the Winnebago manual and see if it had any answers. Of course, it did. It said that when traveling through steep descents, downshift and do not rely on the brakes. Winnie was very heavy, and the brakes simply could not handle fighting gravity for twelve miles at a steep grade. I was still concerned that there might have been damage to the brakes given the amount of smoke, but that had subsided. The good news was that my daughters were done worrying about the brakes and wanted to get moving.

ADDISON: When are we going to leave?
ME: Can we please wait for Winnie to stop smoking?
LILY: I am bored.
ME: Look around you. This canyon is amazing.
LILY and ADDISON: We want to leave.
ME: Please, just give Winnie fifteen minutes (sitting on a step, head in my hands).
LILY and ADDISON: Fine!
ME: Super.

> ## CAUTION
> Observe the engine temperature
> gauge more frequently than normal.
> If overheating occurs, pull off to the
> side of the road and allow the engine
> to thoroughly cool before refilling the
> radiator and restarting the engine.

**Descending A Hill**

When going down a long grade, you may need
to manually shift to a lower gear, rather than
keeping your foot on the brake pedal. A lower
gear will allow the engine to provide a degree of
braking action. Holding your foot on the brake
pedal for an extended period may cause brakes to
overheat, causing you to lose control of the vehicle. See your chassis operating guide for more information.

*Figure 31. Portion from Winnie's owner's manual explaining how to
descend a hill. Information I wish I had before I descended this hill.*

At the point we stopped, we were nearly at the bottom of the
descent. There was just one hairpin turn at the bottom of the hill
(which, by the way, seemed like a really bad idea). I might have
touched the brakes as we went around the turn, but I did not touch
the brakes again for the next two hours. Driving across central
Wyoming was like driving across some deserted planet, but it allowed
the brakes to cool off as there were no real hills to worry about. The
windshield, however, was getting pummeled by bug splatter. I was
trying to make up some time as we still had the hard deadline to get
to Yellowstone.

Eventually, we got to Cody, Wyoming, the last city we were
going to see for a long time. We made a final stop at a Walmart to
stock up on food for the next five days. For a weary traveler, Walmart
is a godsend. While my wife and daughters picked up provisions
from Walmart, I grabbed us dinner from an Arby's located across the
street. From Cody, we were only one hour from Yellowstone. How
hard could this be?

As it turned out, traveling west from Cody put you back into mountains, though the roads were much better for RVs than those we went through in the Bighorn Mountains. We kept going up, and that only meant that we were going down at some point, right? There was a bit more traffic on the way to Yellowstone, but the biggest challenge was seeing out the front window. The sun was setting in front of us, and the windshield was covered with bug splatter. I tried to use the windshield wipers and windshield wiper fluid to help, but that mostly smeared bug juice across the windows, making them even less functional. Finally, the end was in sight. I could see the entrance to Yellowstone.

What seemed weird as we approached the entrance were the flashing yellow lights. I was fumbling to get the fourth-grade pass so we did not have to pay, but there were no rangers at the toll booth. There was a sign that said we should pay tomorrow. Okay. But we needed directions to the RV park, and we had about forty-five minutes to get there before it closed for the night. There was a container of maps of the park, but they were at a height for a car, not Winnie. I could not reach. So, pissed off, I decided to pull over, get out of Winnie, and grab a map. In my haste to pull through the toll booth and pull over, I forgot that if I turn the wheel sharply, the back of Winnie would swing wide. I heard a crash, felt a crunch, and looked in my side mirror to see something dragging behind Winnie. At that moment all I could think was, *I hope that is something of theirs and not mine*, dragging behind Winnie. I pulled out of the way and jumped out of Winnie to inspect the damage. F——ck. That thing dragging behind Winnie was her bumper.

Of course, I did not have time to feel sorry for myself, but Winnie really got hurt. Not only was part of the bumper being dragged by the electrical wires for the brake lights but also several left-side cargo doors were damaged and the tailpipe seemed bent. I am not sure whose idea it was to have large cement barriers extend thirty feet past the ranger toll booth, but to that person, I hate you. I grabbed my toolbox, found my wire cutters, and cut the wires to the bumper. My wife, an engineer by training and who was likely stifling laughing at me, was wise enough to suggest we mark the wires so we could reattach the wires at some later date. With the bumper in hand (along with the license place), I put it on the floor of Winnie, and we quickly headed off to the Fishing Bridge RV Park. We got there with about fifteen minutes to spare.

As I checked us in at the Fishing Bridge RV Park, the park ranger informed me that there was an auto/RV repair shop just around the corner, right next to the RV park. She also informed me that their water pressure would destroy the plumbing in Winnie if I hooked her up without a water pressure regulator. Conveniently, they sold those. Finally, I successfully backed into a very tight parking spot and hooked Winnie up for the night. I grabbed a beer, the bumper, and went outside Winnie to see what the hell I was going to do. What I was going to do was have a second beer.

One thing I realized is that RV people are extremely nice. As I looked at the mess I had made, my neighbor in the RV park (parked about five feet from our RV) asked if there was anything he could do to help. He had a larger set of tools than mine, but since it was getting dark, I thought it best to do this in the morning. He did tell me a more harrowing story about having to escape a forest fire and how the highway they were going to use to get to Yellowstone was closed due to a wildfire. I had not considered, to this point, wildfires. His alternate route cost him an extra four hours. Eh, what are the chances wildfires would interrupt our vacation? However, I did look that night on my phone at a website that showed active wildfires, and it appeared that Wyoming was on fire. Well, not today's concern.

The next morning, we were awakened by a couple of ravens squawking from a tree perched above Winnie. I hate ravens. Or perhaps just those two ravens. A new day meant dealing with Winnie's bruises. The back left cargo door took the most damage of the cargo doors, but I had duct tape. The door was bent and would not shut, so I duct-taped the thing shut. The second rear cargo door was also bent, and only one side would latch. Good enough for me as I needed this one to open as it was the door to the plumbing hookups. The third cargo door was scratched but not too badly. The tailpipe was definitely bent but still attached and seemed fine.

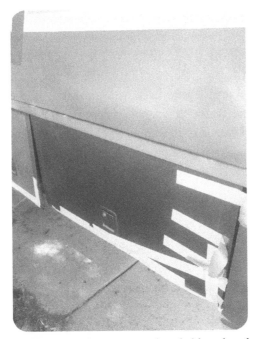

*Figure 32. Winnie's left rear cargo door held with a duct tape.*

We made an early exit to get to the repair shop as soon as they opened. Before my wife and I went into the repair shop, we took a closer look at the damaged bumper. It appeared to be held by two screws, and to fix it would only require a large washer to cover the hole where the screws pulled through. The wires could be matched by color, so that seemed pretty simple. We walked into the shop to ask the clerk if he could help. He shrugged.

ME: We had a little mishap and our bumper fell off our RV. Would it be possible for you to repair it?

REPAIR GUY: Well, let's take a look. Hmmm…(looking at an empty repair shop), we are pretty busy, but we might be able to look at it in about four hours.

ME: Yeah, we do not have that kind of time. Do you have a washer and some wire connectors I could buy?

REPAIR GUY: Yeah…we have that.

I followed the repair guy back into the shop where he pointed at a bunch of little drawers where he showed me a selection of washers and wire connectors. I selected a couple sizes of washers and six or seven wire connectors. For the $3 worth of goods, I paid the man $27, and Teresa and I were back at Winnie ready to fix her up. We drove across the street to the visitor center where Teresa took the girls in to get their Junior Ranger packets. In the meantime, I had connected the wires with a set of pliers and was ready to reattach the bumper. I checked the brake lights, reverse light, and blinker light, and all were working properly (for this, I needed my wife back to check). Reattaching the bumper took only a few seconds because all I needed to do was use my impact driver to unscrew the screws that were still in Winnie, which should have been holding the bumper; put a washer around each screw; and then screw it back in. *Boom!* Bumper attached, vacation back on.

I asked one of my daughters about this episode, recently.

ME: Remember when I pulled the bumper off Winnie?
ADDISON: Yes.
ME: Did your mom tell you not to laugh at my stupidity?
ADDISON: No. I was scared because I thought we were going to be stranded in Yellowstone.

Super, one more thing my daughters are going to need to tell their therapist. I guess my stress engulfed everyone. Kind of like a bad fart in a confined space. Now that I think about it, either my wife or I (I forget who dealt it) let loose a pretty bad fart while I was fixing the wiring. It so befouled the air around Winnie that my wife had to walk away until the air cleared.

# DAYS IN YELLOWSTONE

Once we got the bumper back on, the last step was to secure the back cargo door with a ton of duct tape. Then, we were off to explore Yellowstone. Since priority number 1 was to earn the Junior Ranger badge, we headed north to see the Upper and Lower Falls. On our way, we happened upon the mud volcano area, so we decided to stop. To our right, as we were driving up, I noticed a bunch of bison hanging around what appeared to be a bonfire. Thinking it was a bonfire was a really stupid thought. It was a steam vent. That made much more sense. As we started walking around, we learned that there was a ranger tour of the trail about to begin that would guide us around the mud volcano area, and that checked off one of the items necessary to get the Junior Ranger badge. Oh, and it was extremely interesting. We learned that bison have the right of way everywhere. Every morning, the rangers go throughout the park, fixing all of the damage the bison do over night to the walking paths. We were told we had to stay at least fifty feet from all bison. Bored, Addison and I walked off where we saw a bison lying down on the ground. We walked over and got our picture with him. Probably a pretty stupid idea, in hindsight.

*Figure 33. Bad parents. Stay fifty feet from any bison. Unless you can get a good picture.*

*Figure 34. Mud volcanos had a sulfur funk.*

After seeing and smelling all of the mud pits (and getting the required signature in the Junior Ranger booklets), all of which had their own special name, we ventured forth to see the Upper and Lower Falls. It was nice that Yellowstone had many RV parking spaces available, and we were easily able to slip into one. After getting all of the required family selfies with the falls in the background, Teresa and I wanted to walk down to get a closer look at the Upper Falls. They have a metal set of stairs that hugs the canyon wall that will take you down for a closer look (called Uncle Tom's Trail). The girls were tired of exploring and wanted to relax in Winnie. So we let them go back to Winnie while we took the stairs down and back up.

*Figure 35. The girls with the Upper Falls in the background.*

*Figure 36. Uncle Tom's Trail leads to a better view of the Upper Falls. This sign suggests that you are going to die if you walk a few steps. The steps are a bit steep, but if you are healthy, not a big issue. Our daughters bailed and stayed in Winnie.*

We still needed to get our rental car and check into the West Yellowstone KOA, so we called it a day and headed to the West Yellowstone Airport to pick up the car. I am not sure what I expected to see at the West Yellowstone Airport, but it was pretty small. We pulled Winnie next to the terminal (parking was not a problem), and I hopped out. When I got inside the terminal, there was no one around. Not a soul. Eventually, someone came over. He had seen us pull into the airport and assumed that I was the one person with a car rental reservation. I thought I had rented a larger car than the one we got, but, whatever, the driver's seat had plenty of room. This was really going to suck for the girls.

Once safely connected at our spot in the West Yellowstone KOA, we went off to explore. They had an indoor pool, so we put our swimsuits on and went for a swim. We decided to go out to eat at a restaurant in West Yellowstone. After some Google searching and some debate, we chose Chinese food because that is what you really want when you visit Montana. It turned out this restaurant catered to Chinese tourist busses and not really to non-Chinese families looking for dinner. After a fair-to-middling dinner that took way too long, we went out to find ice cream and to do some shopping. As the sun set, we decided to call it a day and headed back to Winnie to watch a movie, then go to sleep.

On day 2 at Yellowstone, we decided to explore the northern part of the park. We spent half of the day exploring Mammoth Hot Springs, which is different from anything you will have ever seen. Our stay was extended because we had one more presentation to listen to before Lily and Kelsey could get their Junior Ranger badges. Addison had long since given up caring about the badges. In addition, Lily and Kelsey wanted Junior Ranger vests to display their badges, a Junior Ranger backpack, and a Junior Ranger hat to complete the ensemble. It was awesome that all of that was free. Oh, wait, it was not free. After the presentation, we headed off to see a bunch of waterfalls. At one of them (I forget what it was called), we saw a bear family (momma and twin cubs) making their way through the forest. We captured plenty of pictures and considered that a win for the day. Our goal for the day was to visit the Lamar Valley where we were told wolves come out to feed at dusk. Teresa and I thought it would be cool. Our daughters felt otherwise. We found a place to stop along the road, looking across the valley floor, waiting for wolves to descend on the herds of deer, bison, antelope, etc., who were peacefully grazing. Our daughters stayed in the car. After thirty minutes, we finally gave up our unsuccessful wolf viewing to head for dinner.

*Figure 37. Bear in the road in Yellowstone with dumbass jackholes blocking the road. I hope they got mauled.*

*Figure 38. The family at Mammoth Springs.*

*Figure 39. The Yellowstone Junior Ranger badge was a patch.*

There were not a ton of eating choices on that side of Yellowstone. Our only option seemed to be the Roosevelt Lodge. There was a forty-five-minute wait for a table, so we took the time to venture out and explore a path to a waterfall described in the visitors' guide (heretofore to be called Meyer Falls). The pathway was steep in parts and covered with slick pebbles, making the walk a bit sketchy. Further, to ward off any bears in the area, we chose to be loud as I had failed to purchase any bear repellant despite recommendations to do so. We had an overpriced dinner, then headed back to Winnie for the night.

Our final day at Yellowstone required us to pack up, unhook Winnie, and head to the southern part of the park. I was super excited to see this part of the park as it included all of the colorful springs and erupting geysers. We chose to leave early to avoid the crowds. Our first stop was at the Norris Geyser Basin where we walked the pathways around semiactive geysers and got the pleasure of smelling sulfur. Our next stop was at the Midway Geyser Basin where we got to see the Grand Prismatic Spring and a number of other very colorful springs. The payoff was going to the Upper Geyser Basin, home of Old Faithful and a crapload of other geysers.

*Figure 40. The girls in front of the Grand Prismatic Spring.*
*Lily and Kelsey sporting their Junior Ranger swag.*

Upon arriving, my daughters wanted to see if there was another badge they could earn. Good news, there was, and there were two versions: easy version for kids under ten and dissertation version for kids over ten. My wife and Lily went off for the day to complete this forty-page experiment booklet. Kelsey got the shorter and easier booklet as she was assigned to me. To complete the booklet, we were provided with a fancy temperature gauge and other equipment with the task of measuring the temperature of hot springs and geysers. I am not sure what Lily had to do, but she was gone for four hours. We mostly stayed within sight of Old Faithful, and we got to see it erupt from almost every angle. I am sure I saw it erupt four or five times. Finally, after finishing their respective Junior Ranger booklets, we acquired the precious Yellowstone Young Scientist patch. At that point, I was ready to move on; however, Teresa and Lily were desperate to see Old Faithful as they had not seen it erupt. Perfect timing for Old Faithful to take a break from centuries of regular eruptions. After an extra twenty-minute wait, it finally erupted, allowing us to board Winnie and continue our trip down to the Grand Teton National Park.

*Figure 41. Lily performing scientific experiments on hot springs to earn her young scientist patch.*

*Figure 42. Yellowstone Young Scientist patch earned by Lily and Kelsey.*

*Figure 43. "Hothead" Kelsey at Old Faithful.*

# LET'S TRY SOMETHING NEW: SEASICKNESS

Our venture down to the Grand Teton National Park was a short jump from Yellowstone. We stayed at a non-KOA RV park called Flagg Ranch. We checked in, then continued a few more miles down the road to the Grand Teton Visitor Center at Colter Bay. We were lucky to discover that we could get another Junior Ranger badge. We also discovered we could take a boat tour of Jackson Lake, so we made reservations to do so the next morning. Of course, we had to stay for a park ranger presentation because it was required to get the Junior Ranger badge.

*Figure 44. Grand Teton Junior Ranger badge.*

The next morning, we unhooked Winnie and traveled back to the Colter Bay Visitor Center for our boat tour. We bundled up as it was a bit chilly. As we slowly ventured out on the boat tour, it became apparent that Addison was getting a bit seasick. I stayed outside of the boat cabin with her getting some brisk fresh air (which helped her not barf). We traversed Jackson Lake and even saw a bald eagle nest. The best part was Addison not throwing up. Back on dry land, we ate some lunch and purchased some keepsakes (mostly some art and a Christmas ornament), then headed out to cross Wyoming on our way to Rock Springs.

*Figure 45. Boat trip on Jackson Lake. Not sure why I am sitting that way.*

*Figure 46. The family at Grand Teton.*

# WHAT IS THAT ALARM?

The drive from Grand Teton to Rock Springs was supposed to be simple. And it was, until we reached Jackson, Wyoming. We had to drive through the town, which is ill-equipped to handle RVs. The roads were narrow, and the traffic was absurd. Once free of the constraints of city driving, we headed through the hills (looked a lot like mountains from the perspective of this Indiana person). We noticed a bunch of clouds around the peaks of the hills, only to realize that these were not clouds but smoke from forest fires. As we turned east around Hoback, Wyoming, we seemed to be heading straight into the fires. We started seeing signs for Firefighter Staging Area. That cannot be good. Just as we seemed to be getting close to the fires, we traversed a railroad crossing, and a loud alarm and red light started flashing on my steering column.

ME: What the hell is that?
TERESA: I do not know.
ME: I have to pull over and figure this out.
TERESA: The fires look close.
ME: Quick, look in the manual and see if it can tell us what the alarm is for.
TERESA: I am looking.
ME: Silent but thinking, *Hurry the f——ck up*.
TERESA: It is the levelers.
ME: Oh, yeah. It does make that noise when I put the levelers down."

Apparently, crossing the train tracks jarred one of the levelers down just enough to set off the alarm and scare the shit out of me and my wife. By the way, the kids were oblivious to all of this. I got the leveler up, and the alarm stopped. As we got back on the road, we could see the wildfire crest the top of a hill just off of the highway, and helicopters with hanging water buckets were flying a couple hundred feet above us. We got out of there just in time. My guess is that they were going to have to close that road in less than thirty minutes. As we continued, there were entire mountain sides charred on either side of the road. We thought this might have been the closed road that our neighbor in Yellowstone's RV park told us about.

*Figure 47. Staging area for firefighters with smoke over the mountain in the background.*

*Figure 48. Fire is coming down to the road.*

*Figure 49. Helicopter flying in a bucket of water.*

Once past the hills, we crossed desolate and flat central Wyoming. Surely this would be worry-free. As we continued south, I noticed a storm to our west that looked kind of dodgy. In fact, it looked like a tornado. We had no cell service to look at the weather channel app to know what was going on. It appeared to be coming toward us. As we looked at the sky, the clouds did seem to be spinning, but what the hell do I know? I am not a meteorologist. I decided to drive faster and see if we could outrun the storm.

Once safely in Rock Springs, Wyoming, the first order of business was to pick up our rental car at the Rock Springs Airport. It was about the same size airport as West Yellowstone's, but on top of a steep hill, a perfect challenge for Winnie. As expected, there was no one at the car rental counter when we arrived. We waited around thirty minutes, and eventually, someone came around to help. With Teresa driving the car and me in Winnie, we set off for the Rock Springs KOA. At some point that evening, we went out to dinner, then stopped off at Walmart for provisions. We had been running low on everything. I could have kissed Walmart. In fact, I did. I ran up and gave the building a big hug and kissed the painted cinder block wall. Finally, back in civilization.

*Figure 50. Me giving some love to Walmart. Not just a hug, also gave it a kiss, no tongue.*

That evening, I got a message from my credit card that someone had used my card number to charge $10 in Baltimore, and they were wondering if it was me. Answer: No. I called my credit card, and the card had been used for some fraudulent charges, which the credit card company eliminated. The bad thing was that they cancelled my credit card. Sure, they were sending a replacement in seven to fourteen days, but I was in Rock Springs, Wyoming. F——ck me. At least I still had my Costco credit card, and Teresa had her card. But still, f——ck me. And f——ck you, to whoever stole my credit card number.

# DIGGIN' FOR FOSSILS

The entire purpose for heading out west was to dig for fossils. The good news was that my daughter who was so interested in dinosaurs two years ago was no longer interested in dinosaurs. Thus, this part of the trip was solely for me. As for excitement level, I was about a nine on a ten-point scale, my wife about a seven, and our daughters somewhere between a one and three. We headed out early with two goals before we left for Kemmerer, Wyoming. First, we had to get some gloves at Home Depot because otherwise we were going to lose skin off our hands as we hammered rocks, looking for fossils. Second, we had to move Winnie to the Walmart parking lot as we had to move out of the KOA. Really, thank God for Walmart, which is kind enough to invite RVers to park their vehicles at most of their stores.

Tasks completed, we set off to Fossil Safari in Kemmerer, Wyoming (about an hour and forty minutes west). As we got closer, my excitement increased. As recommended by the Fossil Safari website, I had brought two expandable crates and lots of Bubble Wrap to protect our fossil finds. Fossil Safari supplied us each with a hammer, chisel, and instructions on where to find fossils. The process was simple: chip away with the hammer and chisel into the side of the hill to get a slab of sandstone. Then tip the slab on its end and use the hammer and chisel to split the sandstone. In many cases, it revealed a fish fossil. Some were bigger than others. The anticipation as you split the slab and look to see if there is a fossil was addicting. About thirty minutes into the fossil hunt, all three daughters were ready to call it a day. It was not completely their fault, as they were little, and swinging the hammer while holding a chisel was pretty hard for them. So the girls went off to find some shade, and Teresa and I went after the side of a mountain with a fury. We started working together to expedite the process and feed our addiction. Finally, after about another hour, we called it a day. We took our stack of fish fossils to the nice man helping out, and he cut off the excess rock on most of our specimens. I then packed all of our best finds by wrapping them in Bubble Wrap and putting them into the crates. I filled two crates. By the way, we still have two crates of fish fossils in our garage. Want one?

*Figure 51. Sign to let you know you have found the Fossil Safari near Kemmerer, Wyoming. I called ahead to find that the road really would not be appropriate for an RV, especially if it rains. Thus, we rented a car at Rock Springs, Wyoming.*

*Figure 52. Some of our fossil finds. I have two crates of these in my garage.*

As we set off back to Winnie, it dawned on me what a long day we were about to have. Once back at Winnie, we needed to eat, return the rental car, and then drive to Fort Collins, Colorado (about four hours away). It was worth noting that we were completely covered in dust from our fossil digging, as was our rental car, inside and out. As I began panicking about the day's events that still needed to happen, I looked in my rearview mirror to see Kemmerer 5-0, lights flashing.

ME: Shit!
TERESA: What?
ME: Rollers.
TERESA: No.
ME: Yep.
TERESA: Shit.

Okay, that really was not our conversation. I just love the *Blue Brothers* movie. I pulled over, much to my daughters' delight. They thought it hilarious that I got pulled over by a policeman. I put my hands on the steering wheel and banged my head on it. As the policeman walked up, he asked for my driver's license, took it, and went to look up all of my outstanding warrants. Coming back, he asked if I knew the speed limit. I told him I did not and apologized for going however fast I was going because I was not paying attention. He took pity on a carload of dirty tired children and their parents, and we were off, at a slower speed until I got out of town.

When we got back to Rock Springs, we decided to go to the IHOP across the street from Walmart, but Teresa did not want to return our rental car in its current condition. So she sped off to find a carwash and vacuum cleaner station. Thirty minutes later, we had eaten our dinner (hers was getting cold), but the car was clean. We then set off to Fort Collins with a short stop to drop off the car.

Driving Winnie in the dark really sucks. Her headlights are not very bright, and lights inside of Winnie reflect on the inside of the windshield, making it hard to see. Again, I relied on Waze to guide me to the Fort Collins KOA which, again, was a really stupid decision. We exited off Interstate 70 to Highway 287—a state two-lane highway. Of course, it was hilly, and there were many turns. The bonus was that I could only see about twenty-five yards in front of Winnie at night without any glare coming from the inside. This was the scariest drive I had the entire trip, even eclipsing the Bighorn Mountains. There were zero lights along the highway, and I could barely see. The bug splatter did not help. Of course, had I just stayed on the interstate, it would have been easier and only cost us twenty-five minutes, at most. Eat shit, Waze.

We arrived at the KOA late. The folks at the KOA provided a map to our parking space. We wound our way around (at first pulling in the space the wrong direction), plugged in, and were set for the night (after a beer, of course). The next morning, we had to unplug to go pick up our rental car. The plan was to rent a car to go to the Cheyenne Frontier Days Festival in Cheyenne, Wyoming, but at this point in the vacation, no one had an appetite for that. The girls wanted to take it easy and just do nothing. We found out Fort Collins had a public water park that we thought we would go to, only to find out it was closed on Wednesdays. Seriously? Et tu, Fort

Collins? I called my brother (who lived in Denver) for some advice, and he recommended we go to Rocky Mountain National Park.

We told the girls we were going to go to a park for lunch, without really telling them where we were going. It was only an hour away, so why not? They caught on when we pulled into the park entrance and noticed that we were not at a restaurant. For Lily and Kelsey, being at a national park meant that we had to get a Junior Ranger badge…dammit. We got the booklets, then headed over to a restaurant in the park where the girls worked on their books while we waited for the food to arrive. The good news was that it took way too long to get the food, so the girls were almost done with their booklets.

*Figure 53. Rocky Mountain National Park Junior Ranger badge.*

To make up for the crappy small car we rented in Yellowstone, I upgraded to a large SUV when I rented the car in Fort Collins. It was a sweet ride (Infiniti Q80), but it came with some strings attached in the rental agreement, including the rental car company requiring me to promise not to take the car off road. Okay, I thought, why would

I ever go off road? After lunch, we decided to drive up to the top of the mountain. Teresa recommended we take the dodgy way up, which turned out to be a dirt/gravel road up the mountain with tons of switchbacks. So much for the "no off road" pledge.

This ascent—Old Fall River Road—is one of my favorite memories of our entire trip. This one-way dirt and gravel road provided amazing overlooks of the valley below. If you are scared of heights, this is probably not the route to take. As we made our way up, we found ourselves behind a minivan with Missouri license plates, staying as far away from the edge as possible, almost scraping against the rock wall side of the road. Finally, I had enough of going five miles per hour, so I passed the van when the road got a little wider. When I looked over at the driver as we passed him, I had never seen anyone look so scared in my life. He looked pale and appeared to have a death grip on the steering wheel with both hands. Look, once you start on the Old Falls River Road, there is only one way out, and that is up to the summit. I am scared of heights, but I can drive without looking over the edge. I let my family enjoy the scenery, I just needed to follow the road. It is not like suddenly the road is going to crumble away. And if it does, there is nothing you can do about it. So just drive. Inching along scared only makes it worse for everyone else. Whenever I need a smile, I just remember that guy's face as I passed him. Yep, I am smiling now. Luckily we took a picture of him.

*Figure 54. Driving behind scared loser from Missouri. He could not be any closer to the rock wall and farther from the edge of the road and was driving slower than five miles per hour. When we finally passed him, I have never seen anyone so scared in my life. He probably should have gone a different route.*

Once we reached the summit, we got out at the ranger station for a bathroom break. We intended to take the path to the true summit for a photo op, but none of us were dressed for the weather. My daughters had shorts and tanks. We posed for a quick picture at the ranger station and got the hell back in the car, heater on. From there, the trip down was so much easier than the ascent. A nicely paved road wound down the mountain. Our only stop on the way out was to get the Junior Ranger badge for completing the booklets, including the formal swearing in ceremony.

*Figure 55. Our family not dressed for the weather at the Alpine Visitor Center in Rocky Mountain National Park. We took the picture and ran back to the car to get warm.*

# LET'S JUST GET HOME

The next morning, the girls wanted to take advantage of all the amenities the Fort Collins KOA had to offer. We rented leg-powered go-carts and swan-shaped paddleboats and did some bumper boats. The KOA folks kept reminding me that we had to leave by 11:00 AM. With ten minutes to spare, we unhooked Winnie and were off. Originally, we had considered stopping somewhere in Nebraska to go horseback riding, but no one had any interest in doing that, especially me.

FLASHBACK: I had gone horseback riding once before with Teresa's family. The saddle was on wrong, and I spent the ride catawampus, much to the delight of my wife. Since then, I really had no real interest in horseback riding.

My goal was to get home, and the day's goal was to drive straight from Fort Collins to the Lincoln, Nebraska, KOA. During the drive, I reveled in the joy of knowing that someone was going to buy Winnie, and I was going to be done with her, though I knew I was going to have to repair her first.

*Figure 56. Addison, Lily, and me in a dragon paddleboat, crushing Teresa and Kelsey's paddleboat in a race at KOA in Fort Collins, Colorado.*

At some point during the ride through Nebraska, the family came forward and encroached on my sacred personal space.

ME: What is up?

TERESA: Are you sure you want to sell Winnie?

ME: Yes.

TERESA: Don't you want to do this again?

ME: No.

TERESA: There are so many other places we could go. Like the Grand Canyon.

ME: I have never been to the Grand Canyon.

TERESA: See, we could go out west to the Grand Canyon next year.

FAMILY: Silence…just looking at me with sad eyes…

ME: Fine. Next year, we will go on another trip. Then we are selling Winnie. Period.

FAMILY: Dad you are the best! (Cheers.)

ME: muttering

After Lincoln, Nebraska, we stopped at the Quad Cities for the last night at a KOA. My dad's cousin lived there, so we stopped at their house for a while before reaching the KOA. We celebrated our last night with a campfire and s'mores. Our final day started with a crossing of the Mississippi River, officially no longer West. Several hours later, we pulled a weary Winnie into the driveway—we had made it home.

*Figure 57. Last night on the road. Roasting marshmallows next to Winnie at the KOA in Quad Cities, Illinois.*

# HELPFUL HINT: HOW TO STAY AWAKE

No question caffeine helps on the long drives, but it is also helpful to have your brain engaged. For me, my lifeline were podcasts and Audible audiobooks. I had hoarded my favorite podcasts the weeks leading up to the big trip to assure that I had plenty of things to listen to while driving. My favorite podcasts included *The Adam Carolla Show*, *The Tony Kornheiser Show*, and *The Dan Le Batard Show*. The benefit of these podcasts was that they were daily, thus replenishing my queue. I also listened to the Adam Carolla books through Audible. Each of these shows are funny, and it is hard to be sleepy when laughing. I would only recommend that using earbuds can lead to distracted driving, so be careful. When driving in conditions that require hard concentration (heavy traffic, etc.), I recommend stopping the podcast and focusing on the matter in hand. There will be times when you need to listen to the RV and the engine, and you cannot do that while also listening to a podcast. For example, when going through mountains, it is worth listening to the engine to make sure it is not struggling too much. Not being distracted would allow you to keep an eye on your mirrors which will allow you to see smoke coming from your brakes before your daughter comes up to you asking what is burning.

# REPAIRING WINNIE

Once we got home and cleaned Winnie out, the next project was to fix what I had broken. Duct tape was only going to work for so long. Since I had already been in contact with a used RV parts dealer that had an exact match to Winnie (when I got the replacement side mirror), I emailed them to see if they had the back left rear cargo doors. They had what I needed and had them delivered. Looking at how the cargo doors were attached, I was sure I could fix this pretty easily. I also wanted to take a second look at our fix of the rear bumper and the wire connections. I decided to change out the wire connectors to provide a better connection between the wires and use a couple more screws to attach the back bumper. I also decided to upgrade the taillights to LED so that they were brighter as the older lights seemed kind of dim.

Feeling pretty good about my repair skills, I took Winnie back to her storage lot. While there, I asked about upgrading to a covered parking spot. To my glee, they had a covered spot available, and so I decided to fork over an extra $50 per month for a better parking spot (seeing now how I was going to have to keep her safe for another winter). This way, I no longer had to worry about snow building up on the roof, putting the gigantic cover over her, or breaking the skylight over the bathroom again.

# CHECKING IN WITH WINNIE

During the winter months, I would check on Winnie about once a month. The goal was to run the generator for a bit, run the engine for a bit, and get away from my loving family for a bit. During one such trip, I noticed that one of the rear tires was a bit low. I own a heavy-duty electric compressor, so I went home, got the compressor, and added air to all of the tires that seemed low. I also was unable to start the generator or engine. I assumed that the engine battery had lost some charge due to the cold, so I tried to jump start it. Pulling my Honda Pilot up close, I was unable to get Winnie to turn over. Upon inspection of the engine battery, I discovered that the water in the battery had become slush. Feeling stupid that I did not remove the batteries when I should have, I was sure I just cost myself three batteries. Sure enough, the house batteries were similarly frozen. As extra good news, one was cracked.

After removing the three batteries from the battery compartment (which was under the stairs as you enter Winnie), I decided I no longer needed to spend the time visiting Winnie during the winter. The polar vortex of the winter of 2016–2017 had just cost me (actually, I was lazy, and that cost me—it was not like I did not know it was going to get super cold).

As winter turned to spring, one of my daughters started playing on a club traveling soccer team. One of their soccer tournaments was in Indianapolis, Indiana, and for shits and giggles, we decided it would be fun to take Winnie. I brought Winnie home to wash her and get her ready for the trip. I purchased a new set of batteries for her and brought her over to take up our entire driveway. The good news was that some of the branches of the trees next to our driveway had grown back, so I was able to scratch Winnie's side again.

Upon recommendation from the owner's manual, I checked the tires for wear and tire pressure. One of the rear tires appeared to be split. Upon closer inspection, another rear tire had the same issue. Dammit. These were brand-new tires I had just purchased a year ago from the dealer. I called up the sales person at Town and Country RV where I had purchased the RV and was quickly transferred to the service department manager. He asked that I send him pictures of the offending tires, which I did. That shithead indicated it was not his problem, and he recommended I contact the tire dealer he had purchased the tires from. I did just that. He asked that I bring the offending tires to him but not to drive on them. Perfect. This seemed like a giant cluster. I found a local tire dealer, Carter Tire and Automotive, that could order two replacement tires, and the good news was the price of these two tires was almost what it had cost me to buy a set of six. With no other options, I went ahead and got the replacements. To the credit of Carter Tire and Automotive, they recommended I put the new tires on the front wheels, which would provide a better ride and move the current front tires to the back so the four back tires matched. With the new tires on, I drove three hours to the tire dealer to see about a refund. Upon inspecting the tires, he refunded me the price he had charged Town and Country RV, which was only about 50 percent of what I had paid Town and Country. The asshats at Town and Country would not pay me the difference. Pontius Pilot-style customer service—way to wash your hands of any responsibility.

*Figure 58. One of the split tires.*

Generally unsatisfied, pissed, and poorer, I turned the page and began preparations for our trip to Indianapolis. Unlike our last trip to Indy, we did not have a backup car to drive once we got to Indianapolis. Anywhere we went, we had to drive Winnie, which was super convenient. We drove down on a Friday after work. It was awesome that it was raining very hard, and about three miles from our house, it appeared that the windshield wiper blade on the driver's side was coming apart. I pulled over in a torrent of rain, fortuitously stepping in a big, deep puddle, and was able to get the blade back into a working order. Back on the road again, the rain stopped, only to be replaced with high winds. Super. Finally, we arrived at the Indy KOA.

We set off early the next morning for the soccer tournament. I wanted to get there early because I was concerned where I was going to be able to park Winnie. When we arrived, the parking lots were mostly empty, and I found what I believed to be an isolated spot to park, not too far from the soccer fields. I pulled in perpendicular to about five parking spots, hoping that no one would park too close to the front or back of Winnie. After playing two games in the morning, we needed to leave the soccer complex. Unfortunately, one jackhole parked about two feet in front of Winnie, and another one parked about two feet behind her. I figured we had to wait until there was more room to maneuver Winnie out, but Teresa declared we could get out. Inching back and forth for about ten minutes, I was able to extricate Winnie from this spot. I should never doubt my engineer wife. I have learned to doubt my driving skills. The second day of the tournament, we learned to park far away from the soccer fields, and all was fine. All things considered, this trip was the least stressful, so I decided we were becoming an expert RV family.

# ANOTHER WALK-THROUGH FOR ANOTHER BIG TRIP

In late June, we decided to take a trip back to Ocean City, Maryland. This time, on our way to Ocean City, we needed to take a short pit stop to drop a car off at the Cleveland Airport. Like the previous year, my wife had limited vacation, and she needed to leave Ocean City early to get back to work. This, of course, was all pre-COVID-19. Post-COVID-19, she just could have worked at the beach. Generally believing we had mastered the RV, the plan was to wait for Teresa to get home from work around 2:30 PM. Then we would leave in tandem to the Cleveland Airport. Once there, she would park her car and jump in Winnie, and we would be off. We were packed up and ready to head out by 3:30 PM. While the front air conditioner had stopped working again, no worries, we had the house air conditioner as long as the generator was working. Unfortunately, as we backed out of the driveway, the f——cking generator died out. The generator would turn over and run for a few seconds, then die out. As Teresa had already headed out, I had no time to try to figure something out. We just had to deal with it. And it was a hot day.

The good news was that the sky was about to open up and dump buckets of rain all along the Indiana and Ohio toll roads. Heavy rain made driving slow and dangerous; there were multiple major road construction projects on the Ohio Turnpike, and people were generally shitty drivers. We saw multiple accidents where cars had hydroplaned into barriers, blocking at least one lane. What should have been a quick four-hour drive to the Cleveland Airport ended up being a hot, uncomfortable six-hour crawl. The only positive outcome with the rain was that it cooled the outside temperature a bit.

My plan was to get all the way to Ocean City in one day. I knew, given the traffic that existed on a summer Saturday morning to get across the Bay Bridge, just east of Annapolis, Maryland, we needed to get there Friday night. Unfortunately, I was getting tired as we passed Pittsburgh, and I was sure we were not going to make it. Teresa suggested we pull over. I remembered from all of our trips back and forth to visit my parents, there was a Walmart just off the Pennsylvania toll road in Somerset, Pennsylvania. The plan was to sleep for a few hours, then continue early in the morning before it got too hot and the Bay Bridge traffic too horrible. Without any air-conditioning, I went into the Walmart, looking for battery-powered fans. I purchased all they had so everyone had a personal fan to blow air. Somerset, Pennsylvania, is high enough in altitude that it felt rather nice with the windows open, except for the noise. At around 4:00 AM, I woke up, went back to Walmart to get a quick breakfast (Pop-tarts) and a Diet Coke, and then took off east toward Ocean City.

By the time we passed Baltimore on our way toward the Bay Bridge, it was clear that this was going to suck big time. The backup to cross the Bay Bridge was already over two miles, and the temperature was already in the eighties. Inching along in the traffic, stewing in my own sweat, conditions in Winnie were really bad. Eventually, we made it past the Bay Bridge, past Easton, Maryland, with a plan to stop at a Walmart in Cambridge, Maryland, so everyone could feel some air-conditioning and get some breakfast. I tried the generator again, and it kicked on. The house air conditioner ran…for about thirty seconds. Then it crapped out again. I am not a mechanic, but it seemed to me to be a clogged fuel filter. And maybe the front air conditioner was just low on Freon. I was confident I could figure this out and get everything working again because I had the Internet.

Hot and weary, we arrived at the beach. The Ocean Pines police were willing to allow me to park Winnie in their lot for the week, until a bunch of farmer's market pussies got pissed I was taking up three of their precious spaces. I then had to move Winnie to the Ocean City

Walmart parking lot. Have I said how much I love Walmart? In the meantime, I ordered off Amazon replacement air and fuel filters for the generator and purchased an air conditioner Freon repair kit. The Freon repair kit was a bust as there did not appear to be a problem with the pressure in the line. I could not figure out how to replace the filters on the generator either. Zero for two. I tried to locate a small engine repair person near Ocean City to no avail. We were going to have to make the trip home without any air-conditioning. Not having air-conditioning traveling from Ocean City to Granger, Indiana, sucks, but was survivable. No air-conditioning crossing Texas, New Mexico, and Arizona would be deadly. I had to get the air-conditioning and generator fixed.

Since Teresa had already flown back to Indiana, it was just me and the girls driving back together. Expecting the worst, I purchased lots of cooling towels and soaked them in a cooler in ice water to help everyone cool down as we drove. I drove with a towel on my head for most of the way home. I looked like a pirate.

*Figure 59. My pirate look for the way home without air-conditioning.*

Once we made it home, my first priority was to fix the generator. The generator in Winnie was a Cummins Onan generator, and I found a Cummins service provider (Cummins Sales and Service) not too far from our house with an immediate appointment, so I brought Winnie over. One day later, I received a call that they looked at the generator and made some adjustments, and all seemed fine. I went and picked up Winnie and kicked on the generator, and about a half a mile away, the generator died. Same shit. When I got home, I called and told them the problem did not go away and was told to bring her back. This time, I brought the replacement fuel filter and asked that they replace the fuel filter. Sure enough, when I picked her up the second time, she purred like a kitten. All was good, and now our vacation was back on. The next step was to find someone who could fix the dashboard air conditioner.

Winnie has a Ford V-10 Triton engine, so I checked one of our local Ford dealers, and they had a commercial vehicle repair shop that did work on RVs. With our vacation three weeks away, I was confident that they would be able to fix the dashboard air conditioner in no time. After I dropped Winnie off, I did not hear from them for a week. Getting panicky, I called the service manager to get an update. He said they were working on it. Finally, one week away from our trip, I got a call that they found the problem. A relay connector had gone bad. Speaking with the mechanic, he said they spent untold hours going through the entire wiring system, trying to find the problem until he had an epiphany one night, which turned out to be correct. I assumed that the bill was going to be a swift kick in the nuts because of all the hours they had spent looking for the problem, but Jordan Ford in Mishawaka did not charge me anything like what they should have, given the hours spent. If I were going to buy a Ford or Toyota, I would buy it from Jordan Automotive. You should too.

# ITINERARY FOR THE SECOND TRIP OF A LIFETIME

- *July 28*: Granger, Indiana, to the East St. Louis KOA
- *July 29*: East St. Louis KOA to the Crater of Diamonds State Park
- *July 31*: Crater of Diamonds State Park to Oklahoma City
- *August 1*: Oklahoma City to Albuquerque, New Mexico, KOA
- *August 2*: Albuquerque, New Mexico, KOA to the Grand Canyon KOA, via Petrified Forest National Park
- *August 3*: Visit the Grand Canyon National Park
- *August 4*: Visit Out of Africa Wildlife Park and Sedona, Arizona
- *August 5*: Grand Canyon KOA to Page, Arizona (Page Lake Powell Campground), includes a boat trip on Lake Powell.
- *August 6*: Zion National Park (stay at hotel in Utah)
- *August 7*: Trilobite fossil hunting, then back to Page, Arizona
- *August 8*: Page, Arizona, to Cortez KOA (near Mesa Verde National Park)
- *August 9*: Canyon de Chelly National Monument
- *August 10*: Mesa Verde National Park
- *August 11*: Cortez KOA to Amarillo, Texas, KOA
- *August 12*: Amarillo, Texas, KOA to Kansas City East KOA
- *August 13*: Kansas City East KOA to Granger, Indiana (home)

# THE SECOND TRIP OF A LIFETIME IS ON—GRANGER TO ST. LOUIS

As with all of our trips, our estimated time of departure was based upon the timing of Teresa getting home from work. My concern, just like the last trip, was traffic around Chicago. To avoid this, I decided to take the southern route to St. Louis. We drove to Indianapolis, then turned west to St. Louis. It was a much easier drive as it avoided the insane traffic around Chicago on a Friday. However, it was longer by at least an hour. Seven hours later, we pulled into the KOA in East St. Louis. At night, it seemed like we were not in the best neighborhood, but it was a place to park and charge up for a really long drive on day 2. The most important thing I did that night was figure out the best route to get from St. Louis to the Crater of Diamonds State Park in Arkansas. I pledged not to get screwed by Waze and Google Maps on this trip. So I spent a considerable amount of time looking at the routes chosen by Waze and Google Maps, then deciding on the best route for Winnie. As expected, Waze and Google Maps tried to screw us (by taking us off the interstate and through a series of small towns), but I pledged to stay on the interstate as long as possible to avoid the bullshit. With the route planned, I drifted off to sleep. The plan was for an early exit, but we were delayed in leaving because we had to wait for the KOA office to open up so we could pay. When we arrived, it was late, and the office was closed. So we collected our paperwork from the late check-in kiosk and parked in the assigned space (just as we had to do at the Fort Collins KOA). We had to settle up before we could shove off. It delayed us by about an hour.

# ST. LOUIS TO CRATER OF DIAMONDS STATE PARK

It is hard to describe how excited I was to stay at the Crater of Diamonds State Park in Murfreesboro, Arkansas. Years of watching gold-digging shows on the Discovery Channel trained me to be a self-described mining expert, such that I was sure I would be able to find diamonds. The rest of my family was a bit dubious of my self-described talents. The drive took about eight hours, but I stayed on Interstate 55, then west on Interstate 40 to Interstate 30 until finally pulling off at Arkadelphia to head over to the state park. Check-in was a breeze, as was getting Winnie in her designated parking spot. We just needed some lessons on how to get the diamonds, and off we would go. The evening we arrived, we spent some time looking around the visitor center, where they provided detailed instructions and a number of very useful tips. We purchased a few provisions to make our experience the next day better (small blankets to sit and kneel on), but I had brought kneepads for everyone and shovels, gloves, hand tools, etc., for us to use. The next morning, we set out to conquer the diamond fields. After an hour or so, the rest of the family was running out of steam. They wanted to eat lunch, then go swim in the awesome water park that was next to the visitor center. I wanted back at the diamond fields.

I spent about five more hours toiling in the diamond fields. The process was simple: fill up a five-gallon bucket with dirt, haul it over to the wash station, wash all of the dirt (using the rented screens) doing a special shaking motion to move the diamonds to the bottom, flip the screen over, find a few small rocks that could be diamonds, and then repeat the process over and over. Remember, this was central Arkansas in August. It was hot and humid. Finally, I decided to take all of my precious stones to have them examined by a park ranger. It was here that he would confirm that my rocks were diamonds. I was particularly excited about a small bright green stone that I was convinced was an emerald.

ME: What is that green stone?
PARK RANGER: Hmmm. Let me see (looking at it through a magnifying glass).
ME: An emerald?
PARK RANGER: No. What you have here looks to be a sequin off a child's shoe.
ME: Ughh. Darn.

The rest of the rocks I found were equally worthless. I am still sure one of those was a diamond, but the ranger declared it a piece of quartz. The next question, of course, was whether I should tell my family the outcome of my day's labor. Of course, I did and regret that to this day.

*Figure 60. Toiling in the diamond fields.*

*Figure 61. Ready to attack the diamond fields—shovel ready.*

*Figure 62. While Dad melts in the diamond
fields, the girls enjoy the water park.*

# CRATER OF DIAMONDS TO OKC

The trip from the Crater of Diamonds State Park to Oklahoma City was to be the shortest of all driving days. It was a drive through Western Arkansas, then through Eastern Oklahoma to the Indian National Highway toll road that would take us to Interstate 40. Sometimes when driving, you happen upon something that makes you think, *Wow, that looks dangerous.* As was the case as we drove through Arkansas. We got stuck behind a dump truck with huge rocks that seemed to be about to dump onto the road in front of us. Next to the rock truck was a log truck that was swerving, almost into the rock truck. We eventually got past the danger and went about our day.

*Figure 63 In person, those rocks seemed like they would dump onto the road at any point. Better to follow the swerving log truck than the rock truck.*

The night before we left the Crater of Diamonds State Park, I spent some time figuring out what we could do in Oklahoma City even though we would not have a car. We settled on going to Hurricane Harbor Water Park. As we approached Oklahoma City, I saw the exit for our KOA for the night and noticed that it was about twenty miles east of Oklahoma City. Hurricane Harbor was a bit west of Oklahoma City. I really did not want to double back, so I had to find an alternative place to park Winnie for the night. That was a problem for later. This was time to enjoy a water park. As I pulled into the driveway of Hurricane Harbor, I realized I had forgotten to pack my swimsuit for the trip. Rather than considering that they probably sell swimsuits at the water park, I decided I needed to turn around and find a place to purchase a cheap swimsuit. This was a really dumb decision. As I approached the kiosk where I would pay for parking, there was a tight turnaround, mostly for parents to drop their kids off and pick them up. I decided, it was necessary for me to try to maneuver Winnie around this tight turnaround with cars on either side. Like a blind squirrel finding a nut, I managed to get Winnie around this ridiculously tight turnaround without destroying Winnie or any of the cars parked around it. Cursing myself for having such bad judgment, even though it worked out, we sped off to find a Walmart.

Sure enough, not too far away, we found a Walmart and purchased a swimsuit, though not without more complications. The entire shopping center was designed to keep trucks from parking in their parking lots and thus also Winnie. At each entrance to the parking lot, there was a large soccer goal-type structure keeping any vehicle taller than a minivan out. I eventually found the truck entrance for deliveries and double-parked Winnie. We were back at Hurricane Harbor in about ten minutes, this time ready for a day of water park fun.

Once inside, we locked our valuables in a locker, then set off as a family to our first waterslide of the day. The process was simple: sit on a rubber mat and slide down. I was the last to go down and was full of excitement as I hit the first turn, flipped upside down, slammed my head against the wall, and fell off my mat. As I slid down to the pool at the bottom of the slide, I was sure the sixteen-year-old lifeguard was going to give me shit for falling off my mat. As it turned out, he did not, but he did give me a look as though something were wrong. As I stood up, my wife called out.

TERESA: Hey, your head is bleeding.
ME: What?
TERESA: What did you do?
ME: I flipped on the first turn.
TERESA: You might need stitches.
ME: I am not getting stitches.
TERESA: We need to take you to the first aid office.
ME: Dammit.

By the time we got to the first aid office, the bleeding had mostly stopped. The medic was much more concerned about the possibility of a concussion, which I dismissed as stupid. Finally, after signing away any rights I might have for the rest of my life, I was allowed to go back and put my life at risk in a host of other ways. Lucky for me, Kelsey liked going around on the lazy river, so I did that for a while with her while Teresa took the twins off to conquer the more adventurous slides. At some point, Kelsey wanted to jump off a ledge about twelve feet above the water. Not to be outdone by my seven-year-old daughter, I decided to go with her. She went first because I am a puss. As I got to the edge, I stopped.

The sixteen-year-old in charge looked at me with disgust and said, "Just jump."

Humiliated, I jumped. Then because my seven-year-old wanted to kill her dad, it was decided we needed to do it again.

We ventured over to the wave pool, where I am certain there must be multiple drownings per day. At that point, we met up with the rest of the family, and we had some overpriced fried food. After about five hours at the park, we decided it was time to call it a day. The park was closing, and it had started to rain. I did not want to head back east to the KOA, when we needed to go west. Sitting in Winnie as everyone changed, I consulted the KOA app and found there was another KOA west of Oklahoma City by about forty miles. I made a quick reservation on the KOA app, alerted the East Oklahoma City KOA we were not coming, and off we went. One could call the El Reno West KOA spartan, but it had a parking space available to us with full hookups. So who cares if it was just a gravel parking lot next to the interstate.

*Figure 64. The family outside of Hurricane Harbor Water Park.*

# OKLAHOMA CITY TO ALBUQUERQUE, NEW MEXICO

**T**his was going to be a simple day of driving. Nothing to see or do. We just needed to get from point A to point B. I imagined an easy day of just driving on a straight, flat interstate through Oklahoma, Texas, and New Mexico. At some point, Teresa googled some points of interest. Again, my mindset was to get from point A to point B with as few stops as possible. My wife had different plans.

TERESA: You know we are near old Route 66.
ME: Hmm. Interesting.
TERESA: There are some things we could do.
ME: Hmm. Interesting.

To be honest, I was listening to my podcasts and not what she was saying. As we passed Amarillo, Texas, I was informed that the Cadillac Ranch was coming up. I balked at stopping as it was on the south side of the Interstate and said we could stop on our way home. Then I was informed we needed to stop at the midpoint of Route 66. What?

TERESA: The midpoint of Route 66 is coming up.
ME: Hmm. Interesting.
TERESA: We are going to stop.
ME: Hmm. What? How far off the interstate is it?

TERESA: It is just off the interstate. They have it marked off, so we are going to stop.

ME: Why?

TERESA: Can we please stop and stretch our legs at the Route 66 midpoint? We can get a family picture. (To be honest, I do not know exactly what she said, but I really did not want to stop.)

What she should have said was, "Listen, shithead, we have been stuck in this f——cking RV for four hours and we need a break."

To her credit, our stay at the Route 66 midpoint was brief. We got the family picture, purchased some candy at the Sunflower Station convenience store, and were off again. Teresa's obsession with finding places for us to stop and things to do during our drive did not stop at the Route 66 midpoint. My instant response was, "How far off the interstate is it?" and to show disgust at the idea. In hindsight, I really can be a douche.

*Figure 65. The family at the Route 66 midpoint.*

As we approached Albuquerque, I could feel a true sense of relief that the day's drive was just about over. However, there was another Route 66 stop my wife wanted to do. It was called the Musical Highway and consisted of grooves in the road that, when driven over at forty-five miles per hour, play "America the Beautiful." After my "how far off the interstate is THIS?" nonsense, we took the Tijeras exit off Interstate 40 and traveled about one mile. There were signs to alert you to slow down to forty-five moles per hour. The problem was that the grooves were about four inches wide, and I had to maneuver Winnie over these. I sucked at it, so all we heard was the last few bars of the song. Undeterred, I was confident I could do better with a second chance. So I swung Winnie around with two U-turns and attempted again to hear my tires sing "America the Beautiful." Alas, the second time we also heard the last few bars, and I was now convinced I would never be able to properly maneuver Winnie over these grooves.

*Figure 66. Sign at the Musical Highway to alert you to slow down to forty-five miles per hour. The next sign says To hear the song.*

Feeling my failure, my wife then informed me we were going to ride a tram up to the top of a mountain.

TERESA: We are going to ride a tram to the top of a mountain overlooking Albuquerque.

ME: What? How far away is this going to be?

TERESA: It is just a bit north. And it is the longest tramway in the
world.

ME: I said nothing, just thought how much I needed a drink.

I readily admit I am scared of heights. As it turns out, so too
are two of my three daughters. Teresa and Addison have no qualms
about walking along the edge of a cliff. Awesome view: yes. Amazing
architectural achievement to build this tram to the top of this mountain: yes. Scared shitless the entire time: yes. Super glad to get the hell
off that mountain: yes.

*Figure 67. View from the tramway as we ascended to the top of Sandia Peak.*

*Figure 68. Lily taking a picture of the family at the cliff edge. Lily, Kelsey, and I wanted off to get as far away from that cliff edge as we could. Not so much for Addison and Teresa.*

As we pulled into the Albuquerque KOA, we all realized we were not in the best neighborhood. Normally, KOAs are located on the outskirts of cities and towns. Not this one. It was in an "interesting" neighborhood, with the KOA backed up to Interstate 40. As I checked in, they informed me that the gates were going to close and lock at 9:00 PM, and there was going to be a security guard at the gate. I am pretty sure they provided some guidance on how to get back in, but I do not recall any specifics. I was just surprised at the matter-of-fact manner and sternness in which they communicated the gates will lock. We decided on Chinese food that night at a restaurant that was within walking distance of the KOA. My daughter Lily agreed to walk with me. We were both a bit concerned at the sketchy nature of the neighborhood but made it back to Winnie without incident. The good thing about the location was that it was close to a Costco (so I could fill up Winnie with inexpensive gas) and a Walmart (so we could replenish our food supplies).

# ALBUQUERQUE TO THE PAINTED DESERT AND PETRIFIED FOREST NATIONAL PARK

It was a relatively short three-hour trip from Albuquerque to Painted Desert and Petrified Forest National Park. We left early because I had no idea how long we were going to stay at Painted Desert and the Petrified Forest National Park. I had a sinking feeling that another Junior Ranger badge was in the offing, meaning time spent working on the Junior Ranger packet. As luck turned out, there was a Junior Ranger packet. Before that, however, we spent a crapload of cash at the gift store near the entrance to the park. Because I am a bit superstitious and I heard that taking rocks or petrified wood off the ground was not only illegal but might lead to a curse, I wanted to make sure that anything we had, we purchased with the blessings of whomever might curse us. At the gift shop, Native Americans were selling petrified wood, so I assumed the curse was off on this stuff. A couple hundred dollars poorer and with the Junior Ranger packets in hand, we climbed into Winnie to drive through the Painted Desert. Like the Badlands, no picture could ever do it justice. Teresa had the map of the park, so we stopped several times to see various attractions, such as ancient Native petroglyphs. Not to be a super cynic, those markings could just have easily been put there last week, and no one would be the wiser. We also did a bit of a walk, which provided us with the opportunity to stretch our legs and hear from our children how hot it was and how much they did not want to be outside stretching their legs. Eventually, we came upon the visitor center for the Petrified Forest National Park where the final steps to acquiring the Junior Ranger badge were completed, and Lily and Kelsey took the oath of office and received their badge. We also took the opportunity to walk around large pieces of petrified wood.

*Figure 69. The family at Painted Desert.*

*Figure 70. Lily and Kelsey by some petrified wood.*

Upon leaving the park, you are threatened with a full-anal search for stolen petrified wood, but we escaped this treatment with a kind wave from the ranger.

*Figure 71. Petrified Forest National Park Junior Ranger badge.*

# PETRIFIED FOREST NATIONAL PARK TO THE GRAND CANYON KOA

**U**pon exiting the national park, I decided I needed to get a move on. We needed to pick up a rental car from the Flagstaff Airport, and I did not know what time they closed. I had some bad experiences with small airports on our visit to Yellowstone and Rock Springs and did not want to chance it. However, as it turned out, the two-lane highway that was going to take me to Interstate 40 was not built to accommodate an RV going eighty miles per hour. The road heaved in spots, creating a ramp. The first time I came upon one of these mounds in the road, Winnie lurched and bottomed out, scraping the levelers on the roadway. It was enough for my wife to inquire.

TERESA: What the hell was that?
ME: I guess I need to slow down.
TERESA: She did not say anything, but I am sure she must have thought, *Really, ya' think?* or *Hey, Evel f——cking Knievel, dial it back a bit!*

We made it to Flagstaff without any further issues, but finding a parking space for Winnie in the airport parking lot was a bit of a challenge. With our car acquired, the final thirty-five-minute drive was simple, though there were some hills Winnie struggled with. As we got closer to the exit for the KOA, I saw another KOA right off

148

the interstate. Our KOA was along State Road 64, which is the road to the Grand Canyon and closer to the Grand Canyon. However, it lacked in the amenities relative to the KOA at Cedar Pines. I wish we had stayed there as it had go-carts, a big indoor pool, shade, and a number of other amenities. But, alas, we did not.

# THE GRAND CANYON

Our day at the Grand Canyon started like any other national park—Junior Ranger packet. At one point, Lily and Kelsey were sitting with their backs to the Grand Canyon, working on the packet, while Teresa, Addison, and I really just wanted to walk twenty-five feet north so we could actually see the Grand Canyon. Finally, we were allowed to look, and it took our breath away. I had seen pictures of the Grand Canyon, but they did not do it justice.

*Figure 72. The family at the Grand Canyon.*

We spent more time at the Yavapai Point and Geology Museum than I wanted to, but there was a Junior Ranger badge on the line. So we did what we needed to do. While Lily and Kelsey were trying to find things in the museum for their badge, Addison and I looked out the giant windows to see an amazing view of the Grand Canyon. We continued our walk along the Rim Trail until we got to the village area.

Originally our plan was to take a burrow ride into the Grand Canyon. However, due to height and age restrictions, we could not do that. On the bright side, this saved me a crapload of cash. However, it meant that if we were to venture into the Grand Canyon, we would have to do so on foot. This was where I had to give the Internet a big f-you. When the girls were reading about the Grand Canyon, all they read about were people dying or otherwise struggling to get out, after venturing down a trail into the Grand Canyon. Teresa and I thought we could convince our daughters to venture down the Bright Angel Trail, at least for fifteen to twenty minutes. But no. They felt if they stepped one foot onto the trail, we would all perish. F-you, Internet.

*Figure 73. The girls near the start of the Bright Angel Trail. This is as close as we got to actually going into the Grand Canyon.*

Having lost the battle to actually take one step into the Grand Canyon, we went to lunch. There we were satiated by shitty overpriced food at the Bright Angel Lodge. Afterward, we had some ice cream as we made our way over to the El Tovar Hotel for a ranger talk on something we needed to learn in order for Lily and Kelsey to get their Junior Ranger badges. Forty-five minutes later, the girls made their way over to take their Junior Ranger pledge and get their Junior Ranger badges. From here, we ventured down to the Train Depot to take a shuttle over to the Market Plaza so we could do some shopping (even though it seemed as though we had already done a fair amount of shopping). And shop we did. An hour or more later, we took our purchases on another shuttle that took us to the parking lot. On the way back to Winnie, we were delayed by people shocked there would be wildlife next to the road. Apparently, there were a few elk, so OH MY GOD, WE NEED A PICTURE. Teresa got pissed as I just drove by without slowing down so she could take a picture. She did get a picture off before we sped away. I was tired, and when I am tired, I can be a dick.

*Figure 74. Junior Ranger badge for the Grand Canyon National Park.*

*Figure 75. Picture of the elk as we drove by—my wife would have preferred I stop for a better picture.*

That evening, we ventured over to Williams, Arizona, to eat dinner. However, we picked the wrong time as every restaurant had a line, so we went to the Safeway in Williams and got some prepared food which we brought back to Winnie to eat.

# WHO WANTS TO KISS A GIRAFFE?

**T**he next morning, we woke up early for a trip down to Out of Africa Wildlife Park, about a ninety-minute drive from the KOA. It was one of those drives I was grateful to be driving a rental car and not an RV as it seemed like the last ten miles were a steep decline into Camp Verde, Arizona. I really did not ever want to relive the brake burning descent into Tensleep Canyon. We arrived at the park a few minutes before it was going to open. Teresa had arranged for us to have an encounter with the park's two-toed sloth, Bert, and his best friend, a porcupine named Wilbur.

*Figure 76. Teresa and Bert.*

After our thirty minutes with Bert and Wilbur, we ventured over for a bus tour to see the rest of the park. The group ahead of us got in what looked like a nice bus; we got the janky one. However, our tour guide was a hoot. Maybe all the tour guides were funny, and we just got stuck in a crappy bus. At one point, we pulled into the area with giraffes and a host of other deer-like animals. They all had special names but were generally indistinguishable from my perspective. I am sure they are all special and endangered. As we pulled up near the giraffes, our guide asked if anyone wanted to kiss a giraffe.

TOUR GUIDE: Does anyone want to kiss a giraffe?
EVERYONE ON OUR JANKY BUS: Silence.
MY FAMILY: Dad does.
ME: Fine. I'll do it.

Our guide showed me what I needed to do. He put what appeared to be a dog biscuit in his mouth, and the giraffe came up with its giant purple tongue and grabbed it, slobbering the dude. My turn. I got slobbered. Then my wife asked me to do it again as she did not get a good enough picture. This my friend is payback for not slowing down so she could take a picture of an elk outside of the Grand Canyon National Park, the day before. So, yes, I did it again. Like a gentleman, I kept my eyes closed while kissing the giraffe.

*Figure 77. I kissed a giraffe, and I liked it.*

The tour guide dropped us off at the food bar so we could have lunch. I recall it rained on us. After lunch, we were brought over to a place where the girls could feed tigers. But before they could feed the tigers, we were provided a display of why you never want to come close to a tiger. They brought out various blowup items, and the tigers ripped, bit, and destroyed them for kicks (and food). Later, they brought the tigers over to the fence where kids would line up to give the tigers some meat, using those grabber tools.

*Figure 78. Trainer messing with a tiger. Seems like a fool's errand.*

*Figure 79. Lily feeding the tiger. Each of the girls got a chance to do this.*

After the tiger show, we were allowed to walk around and see the various animals throughout the park. Lily, Addison, and I decided to do their zip line, while Kelsey and Teresa went to experience large snakes up close. Aside from mild neck trauma on the last leg of the zip line, it was fun, and I did not have to touch a snake. Of course, the day ended with a visit to the gift shop where I purchased a T-shirt that says I kissed a giraffe. I still wear it proudly.

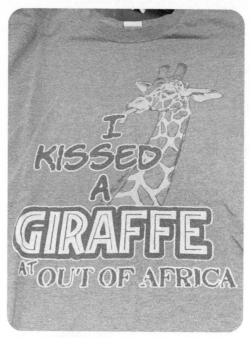

*Figure 80. My new shirt.*

Teresa sold us on the way home that we would go see a ghost town. My impression of a ghost town in Arizona would include desert, tumbleweed, faded Saloon signs, and doors that swung open when the wind blew. That was not where we went. We drove up to Jerome, Arizona, which is a small town at the top of a mountain. Plenty of commerce, including the Haunted Hamburger restaurant and the Ghost City Inn, not to mention the artists co-op. None of these things met our expectations of a ghost town, so we made a quick U-turn and moved on with our lives.

The next stop: Sedona. Holy crap, that was beautiful, with amazing red rock canyons as the sun set. We settled on dinner at a delicious Mexican restaurant. Finally, as the sun faded behind the peaks, we started back to Winnie. Unfortunately for us, the road from Sedona to the KOA, even under the best of circumstances, would have been a challenge given its twists, turns, and elevation changes. But for us, the road was under construction and was gravel most of the way to Flagstaff. I followed the taillights of the car in front of us, and we made it. Bonus, no one threw up. That would have been a bad end to Mexican food.

# GRAND CANYON TO PAGE, ARIZONA

It seemed like an easy enough process to get from the Grand Canyon KOA to Page, Arizona. My obsession was the route. Reading the details of the trip, it appeared that there might be some elevation issues on Highway 89 around Bitter Springs, Arizona. There looked to be an alternative route through Navajo territory, but I was uncertain whether the road was paved all the way from where you turn off Highway 89 onto Navajo Route 20 (across from the Gap, Trading Post) to Page. I decided to chance it and go through the Navajo territory. Even though there were zero amenities, the road was newly paved and an easy drive. Upon seeing the incline I would have had to climb in Winnie (which we drove in our rental car the next day), I was ecstatic I chose the Navajo territory route. Just make sure you have a full tank of gas.

There was not a KOA in Page, so we stayed at the Page Lake Powell Campground (a Good Sam Club—affiliated camp ground). While our parking spot was not entirely flat, the levelers and a few boards were able to get us to level enough. The campground was sufficiently picturesque but with limited amenities. A pool kept the girls happy. We rented a car at the Page, Arizona Airport and decided to take a dinner cruise on Lake Powell. The dinner cruise was a great experience and provided a nice relaxing break from the day's drive. This was the calm before the next day's drive over to Zion National Park.

*Figure 81. The family at the bow of the ship.*

# PAGE TO ZION NATIONAL PARK

**B**ecause we had a car to drive, I was not particularly concerned about the route to Zion, only that we should take the shortest route. Apparently, I failed to discuss this with my wife, who had planned a different route, a longer route. She did some research on the Vermilion Cliffs and condors. Both objects required a southern route to Zion National Park. Though we did not go to the Vermilion Cliffs National Monument, we did drive by it and saw the classic swirled mountains. They only allow a handful of people each day to walk around, but much of the region has the same swirls. As for condors, Teresa found a nesting spot we could go to see the condors in all their splendor. As we turned onto a gravel road my only response was, "How far is this going to be?" Of course, it really did not matter what I thought as we were going to go to wherever she told me we were going to go. About a mile or so on this gravel road, there was a spot where one could see condors if condors were in the area. The cliffs in the distance were covered with condor crap, and there was a sign that had a life-size condor with its wings spread so you could gauge how gigantic these birds were. We looked at the cliffs with our binoculars and saw no condors. With my wife sufficiently disappointed, we sped off to Zion National Park.

*Figure 82. The family at the cliffs where condors nest. But not while we were there. We just saw condor crap dried against the cliffs behind us.*

*Figure 83. Lily and Kelsey stretched out still not as big as a condor wingspan.*

To be perfectly honest, I had heard of Zion National Park, but I had no idea what it was all about. My excitement level was kind of low as I was much more excited about our venture to dig for trilobites, which was still a day away. Once we got closer to the park, the traffic slowed to a crawl. After flashing our "fourth graders get in free" card to enter the park, we slowly approached a tunnel dug into a mountain. It was here that I was happy we did not have Winnie, as she could not have fit through. As we entered the tunnel, I noticed there were openings in the side of the tunnel. As we rolled next to the first opening, my breath was taken away, in the same way when we pulled into Mount Rushmore or saw the Grand Canyon for the first time. Maybe because I was not prepared, but the view and the sight of the mountains through the opening was a shock. As we exited the tunnel and the road turned 180 degrees, we got a full view of the mountains, and my entire mood changed. This was going to be a great day.

*Figure 84. The view from our car as we entered Zion National Park. Winnie would not have fit.*

Zion National Park does not let you drive around, but they have a shuttle system that takes you where you need to go. The greatest challenge was finding a parking spot at the Zion National Park Visitor Center. I dropped Teresa and the girls off and drove around until finally someone leaving had pity on me and told me to follow them to their car so I could have their spot. To whomever that was, thanks. I met up with Teresa and the girls in line to get on the shuttle bus. Good news, Teresa had picked up the Zion National Park Junior Ranger packets for Kelsey and Lily. Our tasks included visiting most of the areas in the park where the shuttle stopped, walking several trails, and listening to a ranger talk on something. But first, lunch. We stopped at the Red Rock Grill at one of the stops within the park. I remember two things about the Red Rock Grill: finding a seat was easier than I had anticipated and the food lines were remarkably efficient. As we finished eating, we planned our attack to fulfill the requirements for the Junior Ranger badge.

The first trail we walked took us to the Emerald Falls. I am not entirely sure we actually saw the Emerald Falls, but we walked long enough to say we did. There were some other trails available where death was a possibility, but I took those off the table, even though I was pretty sure Teresa wanted to go on one. I am a puss and leveraged concern of our daughters' well-being as an excuse not to die. We then headed to the end of the shuttle route where you can walk the Riverside Trail, and if you walk long enough, you can get to the Narrows. The classic picture of Zion National Park is people wading in the Virgin River with vertical canyon walls on either side of the river. No reason to look for pictures of me doing this. However, after walking the Riverside Trail for a while, two of my daughters were kind of done. Lily, on the other hand, wanted to go on with my wife to see the Narrows. I hung out with Kelsey and Addison while Teresa thought it best to risk her life. Again, why am I such a puss? Well, there were signs everywhere, telling you that death was very likely if you wade into the water and a flash flood happens—which by virtue of the number of warning signs, happens every day.

*Figure 85. Lily and Teresa entering the Narrows.*

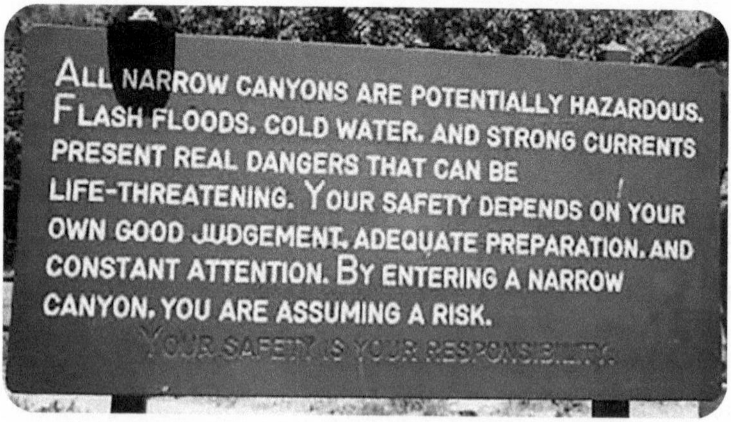

ALL NARROW CANYONS ARE POTENTIALLY HAZARDOUS. FLASH FLOODS. COLD WATER. AND STRONG CURRENTS PRESENT REAL DANGERS THAT CAN BE LIFE-THREATENING. YOUR SAFETY DEPENDS ON YOUR OWN GOOD JUDGEMENT. ADEQUATE PREPARATION. AND CONSTANT ATTENTION. BY ENTERING A NARROW CANYON. YOU ARE ASSUMING A RISK.

YOUR SAFETY IS YOUR RESPONSIBILITY.

*Figure 86. We did not take this picture, but I found it on the Internet. This is one of the many warning signs indicating that you might die if you enter the Narrows. Thanks, Internet.*

By the way, as we waited for Teresa and Lily to return, I began to appreciate another disturbing sight. All around the Riverside Trail were giant boulders. It finally dawned on me that these came from above, most likely squishing whoever happen to be standing around, waiting for their wife and daughter to get back from drowning in a flash flood. While it is not on the Zion National Park brochure, I am certain there must be dozens of annual deaths by squishing. I spent the rest of the time waiting for Teresa and Lily, looking up at the cliffs, ready to make a run for it in the likely event a boulder were to slough off from the cliff's face above us (and of course, make sure Addison and Kelsey were safe too).

It took much longer than we thought for Teresa and Lily to get back to us, but eventually, we were together again—no deaths. It seemed as though almost everything needed for the Junior Ranger badge was completed except to listen to a ranger talk. There was one ranger talk available, so we hoped the shuttle would get us to it in time to have the ranger sign my daughters' Junior Ranger booklets. As we made our way to the Zion Human History Museum for a talk about condors, the family got split up on a very crowded shuttle. Addison was with me, Teresa had Kelsey and Lily by her. We were on opposite sides of the shuttle bus. As Addison and I looked out the window, what did we see riding the winds, but a condor. I really wanted to yell to Teresa in the extremely crowded bus with people crammed in every corner, "Hey, Teresa, a condor," but, alas, I said nothing. Addison and I watched this giant bird circle high up next to the cliffs. We tried to downplay the condor sighting so that Teresa would be less sad she missed it. In hindsight, I should have yelled out. She really wanted to see a condor.

*Figure 87. Zion National Park Junior Ranger badge.*

# NO WINNIE TONIGHT

After stopping for dinner at IHOP (you can never go wrong with a breakfast for dinner at IHOP), we stayed the night at the Best Western Paradise Inn and Resort in Fillmore, Utah. When you see the word *paradise* and *resort*, you think of Hawaii. This was not a paradise or a resort, as I would define them. One might simply refer to this establishment as a motel, but why get caught up in a name? It was a place to sleep so we could prepare for the next day of digging for trilobite fossils. Of all the events planned, I was most excited about this because of our experience digging for fish fossils in Kemmerer, Wyoming. But trilobites were hundreds of millions of years older.

The trilobite site was about an hour and a half away from Delta, Utah. Not that Delta, Utah, is some booming metropolis, but it is the largest town near the fossil location. I love that the website for U-Dig Fossils tells you that if you use Google Maps, you will get lost. Their directions tell you about going to a sign, turning at the sign onto a gravel road, and driving on this gravel road for about twenty miles. Occasionally, there will be a sign that tells you that you are going in the right direction, as doubt will set in.

Eventually, we got to the quarry. We met the man in charge who gave us similar instructions on using a hammer and a chisel as we received at the fossil dig the previous year. We went to the area where we could dig. And dig we did. Unfortunately, the rock was much harder than the sandstone in Wyoming. After about an hour, my body hurt from the vibrations from hammering this black slate. While Teresa and the girls were still going at it, I went over to the discard piles and found dozens of trilobites without having to hammer them out of the rock. We came away with a crate full of trilobite fossils that still reside in our garage next to the two crates of fish fossils we uncovered from Wyoming. Want one?

*Figure 88. The family with some of our trilobites.*

On our way back to Delta, we came across a tree of shoes. No explanation. Just a tree of shoes. We stopped in Delta, Utah, to do some shopping at the Main Street Rock Shop. I am pretty sure we purchased some stuff, much of which probably came from China. There was a general feeling of hunger, but it dawned on us that it was Sunday. And almost every restaurant in Delta was closed, except for McDonald's. While I like McDonald's, most of my family does not, especially Teresa. But it was food. They provided it slowly, but eventually, it came. We still had to make it all the way back to Winnie which was going to be a long five-hour drive, especially after spending an exhausting hour hammering rocks. On the way back to Winnie, my daughter Addison declared she was done looking at red rocks. I had to admit to myself, I had an ass-full of looking at red rocks as well.

*Figure 89. Tree of shoes outside of Delta, Utah. WTF.*

# PAGE, ARIZONA, TO MESA VERDE NATIONAL PARK

The trip from Page, Arizona, to the KOA near Mesa Verde National Park in Cortez, Colorado, was supposed to take a short three and a half hours. Our plan was for an early departure, which did not happen. We decided to stop at the Four Corners Monument so we could be in four states at one time. I knew we needed to get to Cortez to pick up our rental car at the Cortez Municipal Airport and had randomly indicated on the reservation that we would be there around 1:00 PM. Never before in my life, when making a car reservation, did I think I would be held accountable for actually being there when I said I would. About an hour into our drive, I received a phone call on my cell from a strange number, so, of course, I did not answer. Apparently, it was the car rental company wondering where the f———ck I was. When I listened to the message, I said to myself, we will be there when we get there and deal with it then.

Eventually we arrived at the Four Corners Monument, which happened to be on Navajo land. There was a $5 entrance fee, which was a bit surprising, but actually a brilliant idea. A square courtyard surrounded the spot where the four states merge, with different artisan booths selling various Native American products. A cynic might suggest many of these products were produced in China, but I prefer to believe otherwise. In fact, you can see many of the sellers making the jewelry in front of you. My favorite artist was a man named Edward Tso who made handmade arrows. I watched him craft an arrow as he explained to me his process. I wanted one of his arrows but realized I had almost no cash. It really was not a negotiation tactic, but I paid him all the cash I had in my wallet, which was about half of what he originally asked for. I guess that is the game. I just suck at that game. He told me if I hung the arrow over my doorway, it would protect me; the arrow resides over the doorway in my office to this day.

*Figure 90. Arrow in my office made by Edward Tso.*

I think my wife and daughters may have purchased some jewelry, but I have no idea as I was not paying attention. All my attention was on getting an arrow. We did get the obligatory picture of us at the spot where the four states meet, plus one where I was in four states with a hand or foot in a different state. Of course, the sign tells you that you can only take one picture at a time, then get back in line if you want another, but we snuck in a couple pictures at once. Crazy band of rule breakers we are.

*Figure 91. Addison, Kelsey, Lily, and me, each in a different state.*

*Figure 92. Me in four states.*

We made it to the Cortez Municipal Airport around 4:00 PM, about three hours after I had believed we would be there. Needless to say, the Cortez Municipal Airport was tiny, and no one was around. We called the phone number displayed at the car rental counter only to get a surly gentleman wondering where the f——ck I was at 1:00 PM when I was supposed to be there. I apologized for being an inconsiderate prick, and he agreed to meet us at the airport in about thirty minutes. We waited. Apparently in Cortez, Colorado, if you say something, you are expected to keep your word. I love that and felt like a total douche for not calling the man back when he called. Once forgiven, we got the car and headed for the KOA.

Again, I am so grateful for Teresa and her research. We learned that we needed to get over to the Mesa Verde National Park Visitor Center to get tickets for the various tours that were available. The good tour times sell out, and given our tight schedule, we needed to get tickets for the tours ASAP. This also afforded us to be able to pick up the Junior Ranger packets for Lily and Kelsey because, apparently, this was what we do. By coming over a day early, the girls got a head start on the packet while we waited in the ticket line. Of course, Teresa and I purchased some nicely overpriced items at the gift shop.

*Figure 93. Mesa Verde National Park Junior Ranger badge.*

# A WHOLE LOTTA CLIFF DWELLINGS

We took two tours of different cliff dwellings at Mesa Verde National Park. Without wanting to bore you with the details of the tours, I will just say, it was worth it. The highlight was at the beginning of the tour of the Long House when our tour guide regaled us with the many wonderful things the Native Americans did with the available natural resources. Much of what he described was on display in the visitor center. It was amazing to see what they could create with a yucca plant, including sandals, tooth brushes, rope, etc. The tour guide, a park ranger, told us about the specific wood used for making bows and arrows and its unique properties. I forget the name of the tree, but the wood is particularly bendy and resilient. Then the presentation took a dark turn when the ranger explained that it was his favorite wood as he liked to think he was resilient, as he had battled depression. WTF. I mean, great for him, but not everything needs to be about you. When I asked my daughters if they remember what he said, they all told me that they were not listening to anything he said. Perfect.

*Figure 94. Me and the girls while on our tour of Long House.*

The next day, we ventured to Canyon de Chelly (pronounced de Shay) National Monument, which was about a two-hour drive from our KOA. There were ancient cave dwellings here as well, but they were on Navajo Nation land and maintained in partnership with the National Park Service. To get a tour, you needed to contact a tour service, and they would tell you where to meet your tour guide. We met our tour guide in the parking lot of the Best Western Canyon de Chelly Inn. Seemed kind of sketchy, but we went with it anyhow. At our tour time, we were met by a Native American in a Chevy Suburban. I think his name was Henry. Henry took us through the Canyon, stopping so we could see the many petroglyphs and the cliff dwellings. Fun fact, it appears the Nazis stole a Navajo symbol for the swastika. Those Nazis were dicks.

*Figure 95. Petroglyphs at one of the many stops
in our tour of Canyon de Chelly.*

*Figure 96. Some of the cliff dwellings at Canyon de Chelly.*

After our tour with Henry, we drove around to get a view of some of the cliff dwellings from above. We also had to get another, and final, Junior Ranger badge. I was hoping since the Canyon de Chelly National Monument was not a national park, there would not be a Junior Ranger badge, but, alas, they had one. We spent a good hour, trying to work through the packet and get Kelsey and Lily sworn in one last time.

*Figure 97. Kelsey and Lily taking the Junior Ranger pledge for the Junior Ranger badge at Canyon de Chelly.*

As we drove back to Winnie from Canyon de Chelly, it began to dawn on us that we were at the end of our vacation and the end of our life with Winnie. As soon as we got back to Indiana, we planned to sell her. But first, we had three long and hard driving days to get home.

# THE WAY HOME

Google and Waze tried to screw me over one last time. When looking at the route to the Amarillo, Texas, KOA from Cortez, Colorado, Google Maps/Waze tried to take us through mountain passes. Eat me Google and Waze. After viewing the possible routes, I chose to take the longer, flatter route. Specifically, Google/Waze tried to get us to go off Highway 491 onto Highway 550. Looking at the map, you see lots of squiggly lines. Alternatively, if you stay on Highway 491 to Interstate 40, it will cost you an extra eight minutes, but it appears to be a much easier drive. I had no basis for comparison except for googling Highway 550 and confirming this was not a road for Winnie. By the way, at the speed I drove, I am sure we made the trip much faster than had we gone the squiggly route.

Much to my wife's sadness, there were not very many places to stop on our way home. It did not help that much of the first day was spent driving through rain showers. Many of these showers seemed like torrential downpours, which put a damper on the speeds we could drive. The weather cleared as we approached Amarillo, and Teresa reminded me that I had promised to stop at the Cadillac Ranch to see the buried Cadillacs. So we did, and thanks to the downpours, it was a mud pit. The good news was that there was not a Junior Ranger badge available. Just a bunch of tourists stomping through mud to see old rusty and spray-painted cars half-buried in the dirt. Am I glad we stopped?. Yes. Would I stop again? Probably not. Should you stop? Yes, if only for the pictures you can post on the Interweb to prove you were there and that you are hip. When the day was done, I had been driving for thirteen hours and was a bit stressed. I needed a drink. Teresa took the girls on a tour of the KOA where they apparently saw and fed some horses. I stayed in Winnie, drank a couple of beers, and made dinner. I was in a much better mood when they got back.

*Figure 98. The family at the Cadillac Ranch.*

The next day, we needed to get to Kansas City. I changed our reservation from the KOA on the west side of Kansas City to the east side of Kansas City, thinking the extra hour traveling around Kansas City would be worth it to make our last day of driving easier. There was really nothing to see on the way, but Teresa found a place to pull off and view cattle being put into trucks. It was the Bazaar Cattle Pens around mile marker 111 on the Kansas Turnpike. It was a pull-off with parking overlooking Flint Hill. It was pretty, but there were zero cattle. Just empty pens and three pissed-off children who we made get out of Winnie for a photo op. Eventually, we arrived at the Kansas City East KOA. We ordered pulled pork from a local restaurant that delivered to the KOA. Our daughters hated it. We spent some time on the jumping pillow and at the pool. I think Teresa and I brought drinks. Finally, one last night in Winnie, and we would be home.

*Figure 99. The family at the Bazaar Cattle Pens off the Kansas Turnpike. Two of our daughters could fake a smile because they knew it was the only way we were going to get to leave. Kelsey had enough.*

The final day started with strange traffic as we made our way through St. Louis. Apparently, there was going to be an eclipse, and the best place to view it was going to be St. Louis. People were parked along the highway, waiting for the big event. I just wanted to get home. As we passed the southern end of Chicago near Joliet, I had to shit, and there was no place to go. I found an exit and an empty parking lot and did my business in Winnie's bathroom. The hell with the no shitting rule. By the way, I was apparently the only one following that rule anyway. Eleven hours after leaving the Kansas City KOA, we pulled into our driveway in Granger, Indiana. One last photo op with us kissing Winnie goodbye. My next big task was to get Winnie cleaned so we could get her on the market as soon as possible.

*Figure 100. Home at last. Thank you, Winnie, for everything.*

# FIXING WHAT AILS HER

There was no question that our second trip out west went much smoother than the first. I did not crash Winnie, though I almost wiped out a gas pump as I pulled away from a gas station. Key word: *almost*. However, to get her ready to sell, I wanted to fix some things. Highest on my list was a water leak around what appeared to be the water heater. We never used the water heater, but I think that in the winterizing process, I failed to do something, causing a leak. In fact, I would say I am certain that I did not winterize Winnie properly, ever. It was not a big leak, just a constant dripping in the front right cargo bay. I did not want to sell Winnie, knowing that there was a problem that I knew about but did not tell prospective buyers. You know, do unto others...

Who would put cash into something you are trying to get rid of? I would. Because I wanted to sell the damn thing, and I did not want to get sued or otherwise get a bunch of crap from the new owner that I did not reveal a problem. Plus when you list all of the things you replaced in the advertisement, it makes your RV sound much better. I remembered the stress in buying an RV—knowing that we were probably buying someone else's problems. I wanted to be as forthcoming as possible to limit the bullshit I might get after the fact. So am I a hero? Not really.

Eventually, I got around to making an appointment to have it fixed at the excellent Duncan RV Repair in Elkhart, Indiana— the same place that replaced the right-side passenger window. I also wanted an estimate to replace the cracked front windshield. Fixing the water heater and the leak cost about $1,600, and it would cost

184

about $1,400 to replace the front windshield. I decided not to replace the windshield but wanted to let prospective buyers know the cost to have it replaced.

There were also a number of small items inside Winnie that needed to be fixed. For example, the drawers under the kitchen table needed to be reglued, the bathroom door needed the handle replaced, the hardware holding the sliding pocket doors to the bedroom needed some screws to be tightened, and an outlet by the passenger door needed to be reaffixed to the wall as it had pulled out a little. I also needed to reinstall the coffee maker that I had removed because we do not drink coffee and because it was partially blocking one of the windows. I was able to get these fixes done during the fall on random Sundays. I would go over to where we parked Winnie and spend an hour or so, working on one task at a time, all the while running the generator and the engine to keep them in good running order.

Finally, I was ready to put Winnie on the market. I cleaned her up and took a number of pictures to post on the RV sales websites. As the weather began getting colder, I brought the batteries home with me so that I could charge them and to assure they would not freeze. Look, I learned something. And now the suck really was about to begin.

# HELPFUL HINT: FINDING A WEBSITE TO SELL AN RV

**B**efore I purchased Winnie, I spent a ton of time looking at Craigslist. I would not recommend using Craigslist. It is hard to find exactly what you are looking for, and I would expect few real inquiries. I used RVTrader.com to purchase Winnie. The search function worked well, and I knew I was going to post an advertisement here. A second, similar website RVT.com also hosts a large number of RVs for sale. Both websites have a variety of price options to post an advertisement, from the basic for about $35 ($200 for RVT) to the high end of $200 ($240 for RVT). Each option level varies the duration of the advertisement, number of photos you can post, whether it is featured on the site, etc. The prices have gone up since I paid back in November of 2017 as I paid RVTrader.com $99 and RVT.com $129 for the highest level of service. I figured more eyeballs seeing more pictures would lead to more people interested. I was unprepared for the shit show to follow.

As an alternative, you can take your RV to most RV dealerships, and they might give you an offer for your RV. Camping World will sell your RV for you, essentially on consignment. Had there been a Camping World near us, I may have chosen that option.

# I AM INTERESTED IN YOUR RV— REVOLVE YOUR LIFE AROUND ME

I learned quickly that people did not look for RVs evenly through-out the week. Usually, late on Sunday evening was when people were looking for RVs. Soon after I posted my advertisement, I was excited to get my first inquiry. After a few emails back and forth, the individual asked if I could take some additional pictures. I diligently headed over to Winnie, took the pictures, and sent them to this individual. He indicated he and his wife were going to come up from Indianapolis the next weekend to see Winnie. As the weekend got closer, I asked if they could give a time frame of when they might show up—ghosted. Okay, so this is how it was going to go.

Almost every Sunday, I would get several inquiries. Then get ghosted. Finally, I heard from someone local who wanted to come out and see Winnie in person. We scheduled a day and time. Of course, I had to get there early to reinstall the batteries and to get Winnie nice and warm. A woman and her adult daughter showed up. I gave them a test drive, and they seemed very concerned that the screen door rattled a little. After the test drive, they told me they wanted to see a couple other RVs and that they would get back to me. Ghosted. After several weeks, I received a response to my many emails that they had purchased a different RV. In the meantime, I got some felt protector pads to stop the screen door from rattling.

As the weeks went by, the weather grew colder. Reinstalling the batteries and taking them home with me was a bigger pain the colder it got. The next viewing was priceless. A couple came rolling up in

187

a brand-new yellow Mustang GT. As the car rolled up, I thought, *Well, they have some cash.* This could work out just fine. What exited the Mustang GT looked like cigarettes and meth. Smelled like cigarettes. And desperately needed some basic dental care. My guess is that someone in their family died and left them some cash, and they were in the process of blowing through it as quickly as they could. In my mind, I was thinking that it would be a shame for Winnie to go to them as I really loved her and wanted her to go to a good home. Thankfully, they left without ever calling me back, though Winnie had a lingering cigarette smell from their ten minutes inside (which eventually dissipated).

As December came and went, January brought a polar vortex which made reinstalling and removing the batteries even more painful. It also took longer for the furnace to warm Winnie up as I wanted any visitor to walk into a warm Winnie. This was when I had a series of people schedule times to meet Winnie and simply never show up. Hours of my life flushed down the toilet.

About halfway through January, a flourish of emails came from people interested in Winnie. One couple lived relatively close, so we scheduled a meeting the next Sunday. They brought another couple with them to see Winnie, and this was exactly who I hoped would end up with Winnie. She would be in good hands. After showing them the good and the bad of Winnie, they told me they were going to have breakfast, talk about potentially purchasing her, and call me in about an hour. With my hands still cold from extracting the batteries and driving the fourteen miles back to my house, I actually got a call back. They were interested in purchasing Winnie but not for the asking price of $21,000 but for $19,000. It did not take me long to accept their offer. I gave them until the next Thursday to come up with the cash, as they needed to have it wire transferred from a different account. When I got home, I received an inquiry from a very interested and motivated person who wanted to buy Winnie. I told him I had given this buyer until Thursday to get the cash. Undaunted, he told me he would drive from Chicago with the cash on Wednesday, at the full asking price. Sorry, but I gave my word.

On that next Thursday, January 25, 2018, I met with the new owners of Winnie in the parking lot of the StayLock RV storage, where Winnie had lived for the past two years. I exchanged the keys and a signed title (and a couple of other forms required by Indiana) for a $19,000 check. I walked into the office to make sure I was no longer charged for the parking space with the new owners following behind me as they wanted to rent the space I had just given up. I immediately drove to my bank and deposited the check. With that, our RV odyssey had come to an end.

# EPILOGUE

S o was it worth it? I think the best way to answer that question is to say that I would do it all over again. Even knowing that financially it may not have worked out the way I planned, the memories, family stories, laughs, heart ache, joy, and relief were so much more than I could have envisioned. In fact, Teresa and I talk about purchasing another RV and traveling the country again, once our daughters graduate from college.

After hearing some of these stories, I had a friend ask me, "So was driving the RV difficult, or are you just a bad driver?"

My response was yes. I wish I had been provided some driving guidance, though I do not think I would have listened. In fact, I am sure there are books about how to drive an RV, but there was no chance I would have read them. I have a bad habit of being overconfident where there is no observable evidence confidence should exist.

So let us look at the financial results of owning Winnie. On the surface, I purchased Winnie for $18,900 and sold her for $19,000. One might say that looks like a $100 profit. What that does not include are all the other costs incurred. Some were normal maintenance that I should have expected, and some were a consequence of not having a clue what I was doing. Here are those costs:

*Costs I did not consider but should have known about*

| | |
|---|---|
| Fees related to the purchase | $202.50 |
| Taxes and registration fees | $1,694.83 |
| Insurance | $734.83 |

| | |
|---|---|
| Parking | $2,130.00 |
| RV cover | $382.00 |
| **TOTAL** | **$5,144.16** |

*Costs related to ordinary repairs and maintenance*

| | |
|---|---|
| Initial purchase of six tires | $1,349.21 |
| Fix toilet | $566.03 |
| Replace fogged side window | $437.25 |
| Repair air conditioner | $985.81 |
| Repair generator | $246.40 |
| Oil changes | $300.00 |
| Tires (replace two split tires) | $990.66 |
| Refund for two split tires | ($208.00) |
| **TOTAL** | **$4,667.36** |

*Costs incurred because I did not know how to winterize or due to crashes*

| | |
|---|---|
| Replace water heater | $1,626.43 |
| Replace batteries | $501.07 |
| Replace water pump | $450.00 |
| Repair side of Winnie | $1,346.35 |
| Replace side mirror | $223.28 |
| Replace cargo doors | $390.00 |
| **TOTAL** | **$4,537.13** |

If you estimate that, it would have cost around $4,000 to rent a comparable RV for each trip (or a total cost of $8,000). The finances suggest that it was close but still did not achieve a breakeven. We could play the "what if" game and look at the costs that could have been avoided had I sold the RV after the first trip.

*Costs that could have been eliminated had we sold Winnie after first trip*

| | |
|---|---|
| Insurance | $381.83 |
| Parking | $1,650.00 |
| Registration | $180.00 |
| Repair air conditioner | $985.81 |
| Repair generator | $246.40 |
| Oil change | $150.00 |
| Tire replacements | $782.66 |
| Replace batteries | $501.07 |
| Replace water pump | $450.00 |
| **TOTAL** | **$5,327.77** |

Even without these costs, the decision still ended in the red. Knowing this, we would do it again. Money is not everything when compared to what we got from the trip. Having a nicer RV versus the "beater" I was planning on getting made all of the trips so much better. Let us just say that once again, my wife was right.

# ABOUT THE AUTHOR

**M**ike Meyer is an award-winning teaching professor in the Mendoza College of Business at the University of Notre Dame. When not crashing his RV or accidentally stabbing himself with sharp objects, he is attempting to be a fair-to-middling husband to his beautiful, wonderful, and awesome wife and parent to his patient three daughters whom all take great glee in his many blunders.

Lightning Source UK Ltd.
Milton Keynes UK
UKHW042039291122
413043UK00001B/175